COOKING &
TRAVELING
INN STYLE

**A recipe guide book
to the finest inns in
Northern California**

BED & BREAKFAST INNKEEPERS OF NORTHERN CALIFORNIA

Library of Congress Cataloguing-in Publication Data
Cooking and Traveling Inn Style
The Bed and Breakfast Innkeepers of Northern California
89-081034
ISBN 0-9617881-1-9

Includes index pages IV, 1, 109, 110
Copyright 1990 by The Bed and Breakfast Innkeepers of Northern California

Editorial direction by Fred Hernandez and Kathleen DeVanna Fish
Consulting, professional and promotional assistance provided by The Marketing Arm, Monterey, California

Cover photography and food page photo by Robert N. Fish
Sonoma photo by Anne Lee
Humboldt photos by Bob von Normann
Napa photos courtesy of Napa Valley Chamber of Commerce
San Francisco photos courtesy of San Francisco Chamber of Commerce
Cover design and interior color layout by:
Kathryn B. Stark Graphic Design
Maps by Wendy Crockett
Tom Stark, Food Stylist
Typesetting by The Laser Edge
Models: Laurie Mast and Ralph Stanley
Fashions courtesy of Ford's Department Stores

Published by:
The Bed and Breakfast Innkeepers of Northern California
P.O. Box 7150
Chico, CA 95927

Printed in the United States of America

BED AND BREAKFAST - the phrase has two components: a comfortable place to sleep and something good to eat. That's what this book is all about.

Cooking and Traveling Inn Style will introduce you to outstanding inns you can trust to be clean, comfortable, secure and friendly. They are all members of the Bed and Breakfast Innkeepers of Northern California. Each of the group's 126 member inns is inspected by a team of innkeepers to make sure they all meet rigid standards. That way innkeepers can recommend other inns with confidence.

But this book goes further. The innkeepers provide a wide range of recipes that you can enjoy after your travels. In a sense, you take a taste of your trip home with you.

The taste treats include such delicacies as Berry Belgian Waffles, German Egg Cakes, Apricot Almond Streusel, Salmon and Grilled Eggplant Salad, Tomato Dill Soup, Artichoke Frittata, Crepes Normandie, Grilled Rabbit, and Peach Cobbler with Strawberry-Rhubarb Sauce.

And to guide you in your journeys, the inns are listed in geographic areas, with handy maps and area descriptions to help you plot your visit.

Bed and Breakfast Innkeepers of Northern California
P.O. Box 7150
Chico, CA 95927
1 (916) 894-6702
FAX: 1 (916) 894-0807
1 (800) 284-INNS

TABLE OF CONTENTS

Bed and Breakfast Innkeepers
of Northern California

TABLE OF CONTENTS
THE RECIPES

1

The Monterey Peninsula

"Monterey is a place where there is no summer or winter and pines and sand and distant hills and a bay all filled with real water from the Pacific. You will perceive that no expense has been spared."
- Robert Louis Stevenson, 1879

From the tiny Spanish town of San Juan Bautista to the Peninsula of Monterey, down to Big Sur, there are 1,001 things to do in the Monterey area.

Pet a batray at the Monterey Bay Aquarium. Here, living fish are swimming freely in large Plexiglass tanks.

See the history of Steinbeck's Cannery Row or watch whales from one of the fishing boats at Fisherman's Wharf.

Go on the extraordinary Victorian Home Tour in Pacific Grove and delight in the spectacle of the migrating Monarch Butterflies.

Pacific Grove is the stylish beginning of the 17-Mile Drive, through deer-laden golf courses into Carmel - a quaintness nonpareil and a shopper's delight.

And then cap it off with a drive down the dramatic coastline of Big Sur.

So much to do and so little time to do it — you'll have to come back again...and again...and again to the Monterey Peninsula!

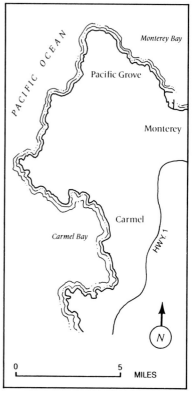

- Gosby House Inn
- The Jabberwock
- The Martine Inn
- Seven Gables Inn

Gosby House Inn

643 Lighthouse Avenue
Pacific Grove, CA 93950
(408) 375-1287
Credit cards: Visa, MC, AE

LOCATED in the historic seaside town of Pacific Grove, the inn was built in 1887 by J.F. Gosby, a cobbler from Nova Scotia. The Queen Anne-style inn features a rounded tower, bay windows, and 22 guest rooms. The Gosby House has been placed in the national historic register. Other features: two parlors, antique doll collection, some rooms with fireplaces, two with small kitchens, marble sinks, and a wine cellar on the premises.

Recipe: Buttermilk Almond Scones, page 140

The Jabberwock

598 Laine Street
Monterey, CA 93940
(408) 372-4777

JUST four blocks from Cannery Row and the Monterey Bay Aquarium, The Jabberwock is tucked behind an ivy hedge. Pass through the hedge and you enter Alice's Wonderland amid half-acre gardens with waterfalls. Guests can be tucked into bed with cookies and milk, snuggle under down comforters and listen to the barking sea lions in Monterey Bay. In the morning, the enticement of Snarkleberry Flumptious or Pifilantro will lure you to breakfast.

Recipe: Cheshire Cheeze Roll, page 159

The Martine Inn

255 Ocean View Boulevard
Pacific Grove, CA 93950
(408) 373-3388
Credit cards: Visa, MC

THIS gracious mansion on the cliffs overlooking Monterey Bay was built in the 1890's as the main home of James Laura Parke of Parke Davis Pharmaceuticals. Each of the 19 guest rooms has a private bath and is furnished with museum quality antiques. Extraordinary features include a 1917 nickelodeon and 1890 white oak pool table in the game room, an 1870 oak steam bath and 8-person hot tub, fireplaces in many rooms, and Godiva mints on your pillow at night.

Recipes: Baked Apples with Rice Pudding, page 112
Monterey Eggs and Salsa, page 127
Sausage Vegetable Roll with Mustard Sauce, page 130

Seven Gables Inn

555 Ocean View Boulevard
Pacific Grove, CA 93950
(408) 372-4341
Credit cards: Visa, MC

IT'S difficult to imagine a more scenic and dramatic spot than
the rocky promontory occupied by the Seven Gables Inn, which
was built in 1886. Guests in this remarkable mansion are
afforded unobstructed views of Monterey Bay and the coastal
mountains from every angle. The eclectic furnishings include
formal Victorian antiques. Each guest room has a panoramic
view, a full private bath and queen-size bed.

Recipes: Two Fruit Muffins, page 155
        Oatmeal Shortbread, page 152

Notes

Santa Cruz

Warm, sandy beaches, gentle surf, spectacular coastal scenery...all this plus redwood mountains, rolling ranchlands and world-class wine tasting is yours in Santa Cruz, one of California's most convenient resort destinations.

A tourist attraction since the mid-1800s, Santa Cruz remains one of California's most popular seaside playgrounds.

Located on Monterey Bay, 70 miles south of San Francisco and 45 miles north of Monterey, Santa Cruz offers a myriad of activities for weekend getaways or month-long vacations. Enjoy the famed seaside amusement park, steam trains through the redwoods or a romantic sunset stroll on the beach.

Since 1907 the Santa Cruz Beach Boardwalk has been the county's best-known attraction. The only beachfront amusement park still in operation on the West Coast, the Boardwalk features over 20 thrilling rides, including the Giant Dipper roller coaster, rated one of the world's top ten amusement rides, a classic 1911 Merry-Go-Round, and a 342-pipe Ruth band organ. The Giant Dipper and the Carousel were recently named National Historic Landmarks.

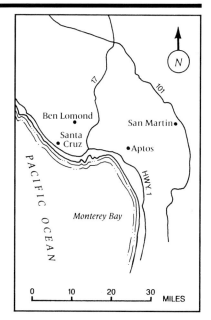

- Babbling Brook Inn
- Chateau Des Fleurs
- Country Rose Inn
- Fairview Manor
- Mangels House

The Babbling Brook Inn

1025 Laurel Street
Santa Cruz, CA 95060
(408) 427-2437

CASCADING waterfalls and a meandering stream grace an acre of gardens, pines and redwoods at this secluded historic inn. Oldest and largest in the Santa Cruz area, this inn offers 12 rooms in country French decor, all with private bath, telephone, most with cozy fireplace, private deck, outside entrance, two with deep-soaking jet bathtubs. Included are a large buffet breakfast and wine and cheese served in the living room parlor.

Recipes: Artichoke Frittata, page 170
Cottage Cheese Delight, page 115
Irresistible Cookies, page 197

Chateau Des Fleurs

7995 Highway 9
Ben Lomond, CA 95005
(408) 336-8943
Credit cards: Visa, MC

CHATEAU Des Fleurs is located in the Santa Cruz mountains about 15 minutes from the beach. Three rooms are available, all with private baths and queen size beds with down comforters. A large breakfast is served in the formal dining room. In the evenings, wine and hors d'oeuvres are served in the gallery or the gazebo. Parks for walking or hiking, horseback riding, antique shops, and the steam train at Roaring Camp and several good restaurants are within a half hour's drive.

Recipe: Armenian Coffee Cake, page 136

Country Rose Inn

455 Fitzgerald Avenue #E
San Martin, CA 95046
(408) 842-0441

SURROUNDED by a grove of eucalyptus, oak and pine trees, the Country Rose Inn is a Dutch Colonial home in a country setting. Features include a baby grand piano in the music room, a swing hanging from a big oak, and 15 wineries close at hand. The master suite consists of three rooms, with a sunken jacuzzi and a steam shower.

Recipe: Breakfast Strawberry Shortcake, page 139

Fairview Manor

245 Fairview Avenue
P.O. Box 74
Ben Lomond, CA 95005
(408) 336-3355
Credit cards: Visa, MC

NESTLED amid 2½ acres of landscaped grounds in the Santa Cruz Mountains, Fairview Manor sits on the old site of the Ben Lomond Hotel, which burned down in 1906. The present inn was built as a summer residence in 1924. The grounds offer winding pathways to the river or two lily ponds. Giant redwood trees abound nearby. Business meetings, parties, garden weddings, receptions accommodated.

Recipe: Eggs for a Gang, page 118

Mangels House

570 Aptos Creek Road
P.O. Box 302
Aptos, CA 95001
(408) 688-7982
Credit cards: Visa, MC

A beautiful white 1880's Victorian on four acres of garden and orchard, Mangels House is situated on the edge of a 10,000-acre redwood state park. The beach is less than a mile away. The atmosphere is casually elegant, with eclectic furnishings. The five bedrooms, which vary in decor, are spacious and airy, with fresh flowers throughout the year. Aperitifs are served each evening in the sitting room or on the porches.

Recipe: Oatmeal Scones, page 151

Notes

Notes

Notes

San Francisco Bay Area

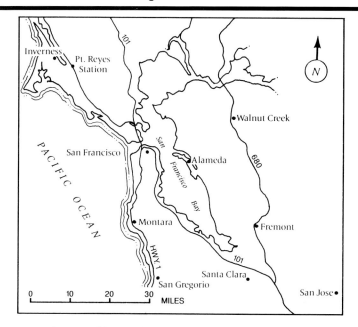

San Francisco and its environs are a visitor's paradise.

A historic cable car will take you past Chinatown, on your way to Fisherman's Wharf.

There are so many things to see and do in San Francisco: the dizzying curves of Lombard Street, Coit Tower, Golden Gate Park, Japantown, Candlestick Park, the Giants and the 49ers, the financial district, Union Square and its elegant shops, Ocean Beach, the Golden Gate and Bay Bridges. The list goes on and on.

To the south are the exciting cliffs of the coast to Montara and San Gregorio. Crashing waves and cliffside farmland fight for one's attention. Further south are historic Santa Clara and San Jose, perimeters of famed Silicon Valley.

To the east are Berkeley, Oakland, Alameda, Walnut Creek and Fremont. The Oakland Coliseum is home to the Oakland A's and Lake Merritt calls one to pause and rest.

To the north is Marin County, with its magnificent coast and mountains.

And uniting it all is San Francisco Bay, home of Alcatraz Island, squadrons of sailboats, water sports, and an occasional stray whale.

- The Briar Rose
- Garratt Mansion
- The Goose & Turrets
- Lord Bradley's Inn

- Madison Street Inn
- The Mansion at Lakewood
- The Monte Cristo
- Rancho San Gregorio

The Briar Rose

897 East Jackson Street
San Jose, CA 95112
(408) 279-5999
Credit cards: Visa, MC, AE

THE Briar Rose is a restored Victorian, built in 1875. Period
furnishings and Victorian wallpapers by Bradbury & Bradbury
grace all the rooms. The grounds boast a gazebo, wraparound
porch, a pond and a quaint Victorian cottage. The inn is located
in a residential section of San Jose with good freeway access,
about 10 minutes from San Jose Airport.

Recipe: Sour Cream Coffee Cake, page 154

Garratt Mansion

900 Union Street
Alameda, CA 94501
(415) 521-4779

THIS Victorian mansion, built in 1893, boasts carved redwood and oak throughout the main floor and balcony, and large, leaded stained glass windows. Six guest rooms are available on the second and third floors, each with a comfortable area where one may read or simply enjoy the quiet. Breakfast is enjoyed either in the dining room or brought to the guest's room. A second-floor guest living room provides games, menus, books and beverages.

Recipe: Tomato Dill Soup, page 166

The Goose & Turrets

835 George Street
P.O. Box 937
Montara, CA 94037-0937
(415) 728-5451
Credit cards: Visa, MC, AE

THE Goose & Turrets was built around 1908 in the Northern Italian villa style. It has housed a Spanish-American War veteran's country club, a music studio and clandestine fun during Prohibition. It is located in Montara, where only three streets are paved and the surf is the loudest thing in town. The five guest rooms include German down comforters, English towel warmers and bathrobes. Mascot geese guard the rose garden, orchard, Appalachian swing and fountain. Two breakfast courses may feature French, Italian, English, U.S. Southern or California dishes.

Recipe: Sausage-Biscuit Pinwheels, page 184

Lord Bradley's Inn

43344 Mission Boulevard
Fremont, CA 94539
(415) 490-0520
Credit cards: Visa, MC

RECENTLY transformed into a bed and breakfast inn, Lord Bradley's was built in the 1870's as the Solon Washington Hotel. Eight guest rooms are available, all with private bath and decorated in Victorian style. Four of the rooms are on the second floor; four are in the adjoining building, originally Brown's Barber Shop. The inn is next door to the restored Mission San Jose. Two rooms are handicapped accessible.

Recipe: French Toast with Orange Butter, page 124

Madison Street Inn

1390 Madison Street
Santa Clara, CA 95050
(408) 249-5541
Credit cards: Visa, MC, AE, Diners

THIS elegantly restored Victorian features 5 guest rooms, 3 with private baths. The rooms contain brass beds, tubs for two and a romantic four-poster bed. The half-acre of landscaped gardens and meeting room can accommodate business meetings and weddings. Pool and spa featured. Available by special request: laundry, dry cleaning, FAX, or special dinners for groups of 4 to 20.

Recipes: Eggs Madison, page 121
Marinated Pork Tenderloin with Orange Sauce, page 181
Special Morning, page 187

The Mansion at Lakewood

1056 Hacienda Drive
Walnut Creek, CA 94598
(415) 946-9075
Credit cards: Visa, MC, AE, Discover

THIS 1861 Victorian country manor is set amid three acres behind white iron gates. The manor features two parlors, majestic library, and an elegant dining room. The seven guest rooms include canopy beds, porches, balcony and a suite with antique brass canopy bed and a jacuzzi for two. Goose down comforters, fluffy robes, fresh flowers, breakfast and afternoon tea on the terrace included.

Recipe: Turkey Breast and Artichoke Heart Salad, page 167

The Monte Cristo

600 Presidio Avenue
San Francisco, CA 94115
(415) 931-1875
Credit cards: Visa, MC, AE, Diners

Originally built in 1875 as a saloon and hotel, the Monte Cristo has had a colorful past. Now completely restored, the Monte Cristo at one time served as a bordello, a refuge after the 1906 earthquake, and as a speakeasy. Special favorites of honeymooners: a Chinese wedding bed in the Oriental Room and a canopied four-poster bed in the Georgian Room. Private and shared baths.

Recipe: Whole Wheat Bread, page 156

Rancho San Gregorio

Route 1, Box 54
San Gregorio, CA 94074
(415) 747-0722

RANCHO San Gregorio is a Spanish-mission style country retreat overlooking historic San Gregorio Valley. Built in 1971, the inn features redwood beams, bright terra cotta tile floors, a colorful cactus courtyard and carved oak antiques. The five guest rooms boast wood-burning stoves, a stained glass window, a clawfoot tub, and one suite with a VCR, refrigerator and soaking tub. Small weddings, picnics and barbecues accommodated.

Recipe: Artichoke Mushroom Frittata, page 171

Notes

Marin County

From redwood trees to migrating whales, from mighty mountains to Indian villages, from isolated lagoons to bird observatories, Marin County has it all.

Situated across the Golden Gate Bridge from San Francisco, Marin County includes chic shopper's havens like Sausalito and exclusive homes on private islands.

But it's the Pacific shore that lures people to a sense of beauty and calm.

Point Reyes National Seashore includes a Miwok village, an earthquake trail and a Morgan horse farm. Beautiful beaches abound everywhere. Some are secluded, some are popular with sunbathers, some are havens for clam diggers.

In winter, the Point Reyes Lighthouse is one of the best places on land to watch whales during their southward migration from Alaska to Baja California.

And one thing you won't see every day are the Tule elk, who are roaming free on Tomales Point after an absence of more than 100 years.

- Blackthorne Inn
- Holly Tree Inn
- Ten Inverness Way

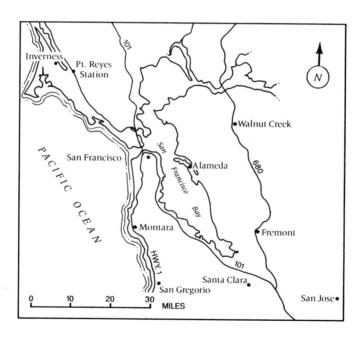

Blackthorne Inn

P.O. Box 712
Inverness, CA 94937
(415) 663-8621
Credit cards: Visa, MC

Sunset Magazine calls Blackthorne Inn a "carpenter's fantasy." The unique structure, nestled in a wooded canyon on the magnificent Point Reyes Peninsula, resembles a giant treehouse. Crafted from redwood, cedar and an 180-foot douglas fir cut and milled on the site, the four-level inn offers extraordinary features like a spiral staircase, antique brass bed, glass solarium and a skywalk leading to the hillside hot and cold tub deck. Continental breakfast includes fresh squeezed juice and pastries.

Recipe: Artichoke and Black Olive Frittata, page 169

BLACKTHORNE INN, INVERNESS, CALIFORNIA

Holly Tree Inn

3 Silverhills Road
P.O. Box 642
Point Reyes Station, CA 94956
(415) 663-1554
Credit cards: Visa, MC

THE heart of the Holly Tree Inn is a spacious living room with overstuffed chairs, sofas upholstered in Laura Ashley prints and a large brick fireplace. The two-story clapboard inn, built in the 1930's, adjoins the magnificent Point Reyes National Seashore parklands. Four corner rooms with private baths or a cottage in the woods are available. Says the New York Times: "The emphasis is on quiet comfort and reflectiveness, the kind one finds after staring into the fire long enough to lose track of time."

Recipe: Zucchini Frittata, page 188

Ten Inverness Way

10 Inverness Way
P.O. Box 63
Inverness, CA 94937
(415) 669-1648
Credit cards: Visa, MC

THIS comfortable inn, built in 1904, is situated in a charming coastal village. It features a country garden, hearty breakfasts, handmade quilts and all the activities of the Point Reyes National Seashore. Says the Los Angeles Times: "One of the niftiest inns in Northern California . . . snug as a Christmas stocking, as cheery as a roaring fire."

Recipe: Whole Wheat Carrot Bread, page 157

Notes

Notes

Notes

Sonoma County

Sonoma County is home to award-winning wineries, majestic redwoods and coastline vistas for whale watching. No matter which direction you travel, you'll discover activities that will make your visit memorable.

You may want to begin your tour in the northernmost towns of Cloverdale, Geyserville and Healdsburg — the heart of this fertile wine region. Lift-off in a hot-air balloon at daybreak or enjoy freshly baked muffins in the breakfast nook of your Bed and Breakfast Inn.

In Santa Rosa, shop for antiques and treasures in Historic Railroad Square or gifts and clothing in Montgomery Village.

On the rugged Sonoma coast, Bodega Bay and other northern coastal hamlets offer fine food and lodging and some of the most spectacular scenery in California. In the winter and spring months, the California Gray Whales may be seen from the coastline as they migrate to and from the warm waters of Mexico. Throughout the year, visit Fort Ross State Historic Park, 11 miles northeast of Jenner, a restored Russian fur trading settlement dating back to 1812.

In Sonoma, visit the Sonoma Mission — the last and northernmost of California's 21 missions — and General Mariano Vallejo's Victorian style home and the barracks for his troops.

- Belle de Jour Inn
- Camellia Inn
- Campbell Ranch Inn
- Country Meadow Inn
- The Estate Inn
- Healdsburg Inn on the Plaza
- Heart's Desire Inn
- The Hidden Oak
- The Hope-Merrill House
- The Hope-Bosworth House
- Huckleberry Springs
- Madrona Manor
- Ridenhour Ranch House Inn
- Victorian Garden Inn
- Vintage Towers
- Ye Olde Shelford House

Belle de Jour Inn

16276 Healdsburg Avenue
Healdsburg, CA 95448
(707) 433-7892
Credit cards: Visa, MC

BELLE de Jour's six-acre hideaway sits on a hilltop with a view of the valley. The Italianate Victorian farmhouse was built around the turn of the century. Guests enjoy breakfast in the farmhouse's country kitchen or garden deck. The guest rooms consist of a cluster of white cottages nestled amid gardens. The cottages boast antiques, whirlpool tubs for two, and fireplaces. Vintage 1923 auto tours available.

Recipe: Parmesan Eggs, page 129

Camellia Inn

211 North Street
Healdsburg, CA 95448
(707) 433-8182
Credit cards: Visa, MC

BUILT in 1869, the Camellia Inn is an elegant Italianate Victorian townhouse. Features include antiques, inlaid hardwood floors, chandeliers and Oriental rugs. Horticulturist Luther Burbank was a friend of an early owner, and many of the 30 varieties of camellias on the grounds are attributed to him. Other features: double parlors with twin marble fireplaces, villa-styled swimming pool, whirlpool tub and gas fireplaces in some rooms.

Recipe: Huevos Mexicanos, page 178

Campbell Ranch Inn

1475 Canyon Road
Geyserville, CA 95441
(707) 857-3476
Credit cards: Visa, MC

THIS hilltop inn, set amid 35 country acres, overlooks the rolling vineyards of Sonoma County. Guests have the use of swimming pool, hot tub, spa, tennis court, bicycles, ping pong and horseshoes. The garden's abundant flowers are a photographer's dream. The five guest rooms boast king-size beds and private baths, and most have a balcony. Provided are a full breakfast, fruit and flowers in the rooms, and homemade pie or cake in the evenings.

Recipe: Chinese Cabbage Salad, page 163

Country Meadow Inn

11360 Old Redwood Highway
Windsor, CA 95492
(707) 431-1276
Credit cards: Visa, MC

LOCATED in the heart of the Sonoma County wine region, Country Meadow Inn is a restored 1890 Queen Anne Victorian farmhouse. The inn's furnishings are a blend of country and Victorian antiques. The five guest rooms include private baths and whirlpool tubs. The pool, decks and flower beds display wildflowers, seasonal bulbs or roses framed with redwood arches or stone walls, recently described by a guest as "a painting created with love."

Recipe: Fresh Fruit Coffeecake, page 144

The Estate Inn

13555 Highway 116
Guerneville, CA 95446
(707) 869-9093
Credit cards: Visa, MC, AE

DEVELOPED in 1922 by a flamboyant banker, The Estate is located in the Russian River Valley, minutes from wineries, tidepools, cabarets, mudbaths, giant redwoods and the dramatic Sonoma Coast. Dinner is now being served at The Estate. Cooking skills were learned in such wide-ranging places as the Thai Cooking School in Bangkok and the Ristorante Parco Ciani in Lugano. Most of the produce comes from The Estate's gardens.

Recipe: Leg of Lamb with Pistachio Nut Stuffing, page 179

Healdsburg Inn on the Plaza

116 Matheson Street
P.O. Box 1196
Healdsburg, CA 95448
(707) 433-6991
Credit cards: Visa, MC, AE

THE historic Wells Fargo building of 1900 has been transformed into a unique inn. The lower floor contains two gift shops, a bakery and an art gallery. A grand staircase in the art gallery leads to the guest rooms, all with queen beds, private baths, some with fireplaces. The inn also boasts a solarium with resident lovebirds and a roof garden.

Recipe: Nutty Oat Wheat Bread, page 149

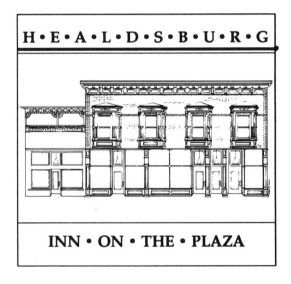

H • E • A • L • D • S • B • U • R • G

INN • ON • THE • PLAZA

Heart's Desire Inn

3657 Church Street
P.O. Box 857
Occidental, CA 95465
(707) 874-1311
Credit cards: Visa, MC, AE

THIS restored two-story Victorian, built in 1867, is nestled in the redwoods near the spectacular Sonoma County coast and wine country. The inn features antique pine furnishings, goose-down comforters and large European-style pillows. A walled garden contains a moss-mantled fountain. The town of Occidental features antique and handicrafts shops, and hearty Italian restaurants.

Recipe: Peach Cobbler with Strawberry-Rhubarb Sauce, page 199

The Hidden Oak

214 East Napa Street
Sonoma, CA 95476
(707) 996-9863
Credit cards: AE

BUILT in 1913, this large, two-story house is a restored California Craftsman Bungalow. The three guest rooms feature antiques and wicker furniture, private baths and comfortable beds. Located within walking distance of the Plaza, a state and national landmark, The Hidden Oak offers bicycles so guests can visit the Mission, restaurants, wineries and theaters.

Recipe: Sonoma Sunrise Bread, page 153

The Hope-Merrill and Hope-Bosworth House

21253 Geyserville Avenue
P.O. Box 42
Geyserville, CA 95441
(707) 857-3356
Credit cards: Visa, MC, AE

THESE vintage, turn-of-the-century Victorians face each other amid the premium wine country. The charming houses offer 12 guest rooms, private baths (two with whirlpool jacuzzis), beautiful Victorian gardens, vineyards and a heated swimming pool. Featured in Country Homes, Sunset, House Beautiful and Los Angeles Times. The inns offer a grand view of Geyser Peak, the world's largest geothermal field.

Recipe: Coffee Cake Supreme, page 141

Huckleberry Springs Country Inn

8105 Old Beedle Road
P.O. Box 400
Monte Rio, CA 95462
(707) 865-2683
Credit cards: Visa, MC, AE

LOCATED on 56 acres above the Russian River, Huckleberry Springs offers a hillside spa, swimming pool and gourmet dining in a solarium under the redwoods. The kitchen specializes in varied cuisine using fresh seasonal produce, seafoods and fine wines of Sonoma. Four unique cottages offer private baths, skylights and woodstoves. Breakfast and dinner included daily.

Recipe: Salmon and Grilled Eggplant Salad, page 164

Madrona Manor

1001 Westside Road
P.O. Box 818
Healdsburg, CA 95448
(707) 433-4231
Credit cards: Visa, MC, AE, Diners

BUILT in 1881, this majestic three-story mansion is surrounded by eight acres of wooded and landscaped grounds. The mansion offers 18 rooms and 2 suites, all with private baths. The main house features an original rosewood piano and fireplaces in the guest rooms. The carriage house, lavish with hand-carved rosewood, also contains a billiard table. Chef Todd Muir was trained at the California Culinary Academy and famed Chez Panisse.

Recipe: Poulet Saute Aux Olives de Provence, page 183

Ridenhour Ranch House Inn

12850 River Road
Guerneville, CA 95446
(707) 887-1033
Credit cards: Visa, MC

CONSTRUCTED in 1906 of heart redwood, this handsome ranch house is surrounded by 2½ acres of redwoods, oaks and madrones. A cottage and guest rooms feature a stained glass wisteria window, queen-size Victorian bed, and fireplace. A hot tub is available. Close to the Russian River, redwood state park, coastal beaches. The Korbel Champagne cellars are within walking distance. Gourmet dinners are available.

Recipe: Applesauce Cake, page 193

Victorian Garden Inn

316 East Napa Street
Sonoma, CA 95476
(707) 996-5339
Credit cards: Visa, MC, AE

LOCATED within walking distance of historic Sonoma Plaza, Victorian Garden Inn offers four rooms, three with private entrances and baths, flanking luxurious gardens and a sparkling stream. Guests can socialize by the pool, over refreshments on the patio, by the fireside in the parlor, or in their rooms overlooking a maze of garden paths. Massage services are available, as are hot air ballooning, rides on biplanes and wine-tasting limo tours.

Recipe: Croissants and Prawns, page 175

Vintage Towers

302 North Main Street
Cloverdale, CA 95425
(707) 894-4535
FAX: (707) 894-5827
Credit cards: Visa, MC, AE

THIS lovely Queen Anne Victorian mansion, built in 1913, boasts three towers: one round, one square, one octagonal. The three tower suites include private sitting areas, and private baths. Another room includes a collection of games and antique toys. A complimentary bottle of wine awaits guests, as do three parlors and a 40-foot veranda with a swing and comfortable chairs.

Recipe: Raspberry and Blackberry Biscuit Pudding, page 201

Ye Olde Shelford House

29955 River Road
Cloverdale, CA 95425
(707) 894-5956
Credit cards: Visa, MC

THIS stately Victorian charmer, circa 1885, offers three guest rooms with lots of windows and window seats for viewing surrounding vineyards. Rooms are furnished in family antiques and homemade quilts. A stone's throw from the Russian River, the inn operates a turn-of-the-century surrey for rides to nearby wineries. Also offered: a bicycle built for two, ten speed bikes, hot tub and swimming pool.

Recipe: Eggs Florentine, page 117

Notes

Napa Valley

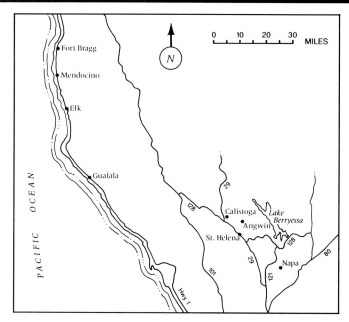

The Napa Valley is a true four-seasons destination. The spring finds the vines just awakening from their winter slumber to the bright mustard at their trunks. This seasonal show begins late in January when nearly everywhere else is still in winter's grasp.

Summer comes to the vineyards in late May, turning buds to grapes. By fall, the dark green vines turn crimson and yellow and the excitement of the harvest begins. This is high season with festivals and parties.

November rains herald winter's return with cooler temperatures and the holidays just around the corner. Hot mulled wine and crackling fires warm the inns to a cozy glow. No matter when you come, the Napa Valley is waiting with surprises and joys to turn into memories.

And your Bed and Breakfast Innkeeper is your guide to these wonders. After a sumptuous breakfast you'll be told of century old wineries and quiet country lanes known only to the locals. You'll see this world-famous wine country as an honored guest, not a typical tourist.

- The Ambrose Bierce House
- Beazley House
- Chestelson House
- Foothill House
- Forest Manor
- The Napa Inn
- Oliver House
- Scarlett's Country Inn
- Silver Rose Inn

The Ambrose Bierce House

1515 Main Street
St. Helena, CA 94574
(707) 963-3003
Credit cards: AE

AMBROSE Bierce - writer, poet, essayist, editor, curmudgeon and author of "The Devil's Dictionary" - vanished mysteriously in Mexico in 1913. His former home, built in 1972, features bedroom suites furnished with antiques, queen-size brass beds and armoires. Bathrooms boast brass fittings, clawfoot tubs and showers.

Recipe: Caramelized Pears, page 194

Beazley House

1910 First Street
Napa, CA 94559
(707) 257-1649
Credit cards: Visa, MC, AE, Discover

NAPA'S first bed and breakfast inn, Beazley House is a chocolate brown mansion. The main house features a stained glass entry, inlaid floors, a music room and a huge fireplace. The mansion's old carriage house has been reproduced and also contains guest rooms with private spas. The manager says you'll sense the hospitality the moment you stroll up the curved walk past the lawns and gardens.

Recipe: Potato Pie, page 182

Chestelson House

1417 Kearney Street
St. Helena, CA 94574
(707) 963-2238

A Victorian amid a quiet, residential neighborhood, Chestelson House boasts a wraparound porch, queen size beds and private or semi-private baths with tubs and showers. The innkeeper draws on her experience as a caterer and cooking teacher to produce a tempting family-style breakfast. The atmosphere is light and friendly.

Recipe: Sausage Frittata, page 185

Foothill House

3037 Foothill Boulevard
Calistoga, CA 94515
(707) 942-6933
Credit cards: Visa, MC

FOOTHILL House is "the most romantic inn of the Napa Valley," according to the Chicago Tribune. A former farmhouse, the inn's suites are decorated with antiques. Each room has a private bath and entrance, queen-size beds, a wood-burning fireplace and a small refrigerator. The innkeepers pride themselves on acting as a personal concierge for their guests.

Recipe: Foccacia, page 161

Forest Manor

415 Cold Springs Road
Angwin, CA 94508
(707) 965-3538
Credit cards: Visa, MC

THIS secluded 20-acre estate features a three-story English Tudor manor furnished with English antiques, Persian carpets and oriental artifacts. Travel writers have called Forest Manor "one of the most romantic country inns" and "a small exclusive resort." The manor features fireplaces, verandas, a 53-foot pool, spas and spacious suites with private baths, oversize beds, refrigerators and coffee makers. The honeymoon suite boasts a private jacuzzi for two.

Recipe: Baked Beans, page 172

Forest Manor
415 Cold Springs Road
Angwin, California 94508

(707) 965-3538
above Napa Valley

The Napa Inn

1137 Warren Street
Napa, CA 94559
(707) 257-1444
Credit cards: Visa, MC

THE Napa Inn is a beautiful Queen Anne Victorian home built in 1899. The inn is located on a quiet residential street in the old, historical section of Napa. Furnished with Victorian antiques, the inn features spacious rooms, each with a queen or king-size bed and private bath. Refreshments are served every afternoon and a full breakfast in the morning in the formal dining room.

Recipe: Lemon Yogurt Bread, page 147

Oliver House

2970 Silverado Trail
St. Helena, CA 94574
(707) 963-4089
Credit cards: Visa, MC

OVERLOOKING the vineyards of Napa Valley, Oliver House is a farmhouse built to reflect the Swiss and English roots of the owners. Guest rooms feature an ornate 115-year-old brass bed, antiques, fireplaces and balconies. Breakfast is served on a balcony on warm days, in the cheery country kitchen on cooler days. One guest called it "the best of both worlds, Switzerland and Napa Valley."

Recipe: Swiss Baked Eggs, page 131

Scarlett's Country Inn

3918 Silverado Trail, North
Calistoga, CA 94515
(707) 942-6669
Credit cards: Visa, MC

AN Intimate retreat tucked away in a small canyon, Scarlett's
Country Inn features three well-appointed suites amid lawns
and tall pines, overlooking the vineyards. All have private
entrances, private baths, and queen-size beds. The swimming
pool is set on the edge of a forest. Breakfast may be enjoyed
poolside under the apple trees or in the guest's sitting room.
Children accepted at no charge.

Recipe: Shrimp and Rice Curry Salad, page 165

Silver Rose Inn

351 Rosedale Road
Calistoga, CA 94515
(707) 942-9581
Credit cards: Visa, MC, AE

SITUATED on an oak-studded knoll, the Silver Rose Inn features a gentle waterfall that feeds into a swimming pool carved out of the rock hillside, a rock garden, jacuzzi, gazebo and hundreds of rose bushes. Each of the five guest rooms is decorated in a distinctive style, from turn-of-the-century to Oriental. The gathering room features a fireplace, Oriental rugs and a nearby reading nook.

Recipe: Hawaiian Bread, page 145

Notes

Mendocino County and the Northcoast

California's Northcoast is an area of great natural beauty with its scenic, rugged shoreline and headlands. Here, one finds the quaint Victorian village of Mendocino, and its Historical Preservation District as the focal point. Its many gallery shops and inns offer unique lodging opportunities, and a number of the finest restaurants in Northern California.

Long a favorite of film makers and TV producers, Mendocino enjoys an unusually high devotion to the arts, with little theatre through eight months of the year, a highly acclaimed annual 10 day music festival, semiannual antique shows, and wine and art auctions.

A few minutes away are the Mendocino Coast Botanical Gardens, and wide-ranging activities including walking/hiking in four State parks, canoeing and kayaking on a tidal river, horseback riding along the beach, golf and tennis. From December to April of each year the annual whale migration is another popular event.

Mendocino is situated 145 miles north of San Francisco, with the most direct route requiring $3^1/_4$-$3^1/_2$ hours up Highway 101 to Highway 128 just north of Cloverdale, then west to the coast past the wineries of the beautiful Anderson Valley, and through many lovely groves of coastal redwoods.

The longer trip of a least 5 hours up Coast Highway 1 goes through the communities of Gualala, with its annual summer Art in the Redwoods Festival, and Elk, where additional inns are found.

From the east, Mendocino is located but 4 hours from Sacramento and 3 hours from the heart of the famed Napa Valley.

- Agate Cove Inn
- Elk Cove Inn
- The Grey Whale Inn
- Harbor House Inn by the Sea
- The Headlands Inn
- Joshua Grindle Inn
- Whale Watch Inn

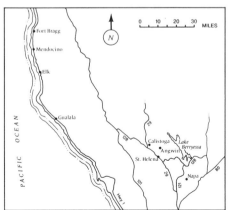

Agate Cove Inn

11201 North Lansing Street
P.O. Box 1150
Mendocino, CA 95460
(707) 937-0551
1-(800) 527-3111 in Northern California
Credit cards: Visa, MC, AE

SITUATED on an ocean bluff, the old farmhouse appears today much as it did in the 1860's. It is surrounded by ten guest cottages and beautifully landscaped gardens to form a charming, tiny Cape Cod-like "village." The cottages feature country decor fireplaces and spectacular ocean views. A full country breakfast cooked on an old wood stove is served in the main house overlooking the crashing waves below.

Recipe: Granola Crunch, page 126

Elk Cove Inn

6300 South Highway 1
P.O. Box 367
Elk, CA 95432
(707) 877-3321

THIS 1883 Victorian is nestled in peaceful seclusion atop a bluff with spectacular ocean views from cabins and dining room. A full gourmet breakfast of German/French specialties is served daily. Beds have the subtle luxury of sun-dried linens. Dramatic ocean views from large bay windows; high-beamed ceilings, skylights and Victorian fireplaces. Ready access to driftwood-strewn beach below. Relaxed, romantic atmosphere.

Recipe: German Egg Cakes (Eierkuchen), page 125

The Grey Whale Inn

615 North Main Street
Fort Bragg, CA 95437
(707) 964-0640
1-(800) 382-7244 (California only)
Credit cards: Visa, MC, AE

BUILT in 1915 of old-growth redwood, this stately historic building served as a hospital until 1971. Generous use of local art graces the inn. Some rooms boast ocean views, others overlook the town and hills; a romantic favorite is the Fireside Rendezvous Room. Beaches, restaurants, shops, redwoods, and the famous Skunk Train are a short stroll away. Secluded beaches offer tidepools, sights of whales and harbor seals.

Recipe: Fancy Egg Scramble, page 122

Harbor House Inn by the Sea

5600 South Highway 1
P.O. Box 369
Elk, CA 95432
(707) 877-3203

ON a bluff overlooking the spectacular Mendocino coast, Harbor House was built in 1916 by a lumber company as an executive residence and guest house. Built entirely of redwood from nearby forests, the inn is an enlarged version of "The Home of Redwood" at the 1915 Panama-Pacific International Exposition. The sea and rock arches are visible from most main house rooms and blufftop cottages. Extra features include dining with a view, a private beach and paths edged with wildflowers.

Recipe: Oriental Ginger Pork, page 180

Harbor House Inn
Elk, California

The Headlands Inn

Corner of Howard and Albion Streets
P.O. Box 132
Mendocino, CA 95460
(707) 937-4431

THE Headlands Inn, an 1868 Victorian that began as the town's barbershop, is located within Mendocino's Historical Preservation District. The five rooms, including a cottage, all have fireplaces, king or queen-size beds and private baths. Some rooms offer ocean views overlooking the English-style garden. Full gourmet breakfasts, served directly to each room, include entrees that change daily. The inn features two parlors and many unusual antiques.

Recipes: Florentine Ham Rolls, page 176
Eggs Gruyere with Savory Garnish, page 120

Joshua Grindle Inn

44800 Little Lake Road
P.O. Box 647
Mendocino, CA 95460
(707) 937-4143
Credit cards: Visa, MC, AE

BUILT in 1879 by Joshua Grindle, the town banker, the inn sits on a knoll overlooking the ocean, a bay and the village of Mendocino. The inn's ten guest rooms are furnished with 18th and 19th century American antiques, including pewter cupboards, early American lighting systems and hand-made quilts. Some rooms boast ocean views, a four-poster double bed and fireplaces. An English-style breakfast is served in the dining room's long, narrow harvest table, circa 1830.

Recipe: Baked Pears with Yogurt, page 113

Whale Watch Inn

35100 Highway 1
Gualala, CA 95445
(707) 884-3667
Credit cards: Visa, MC, AE

BUILT on two cliffside acres overlooking Anchor Bay, Whale Watch Inn offers luxury, privacy and modern architecture. The inn includes five buildings with a total of 18 guest rooms with ocean views, private baths and deck area. Most have fireplaces and whirlpool baths. The location allows guests to escape much coastal fog. Continental breakfast is served to guests in their rooms.

Recipe: Apple Crisp, page 191

The High Sierra

If you're looking for mountain peace and country privacy, the High Sierra is just right. The area abounds in historic sites, majestic mountain peaks, trout ponds galore, tall pines and quaking aspens.

Towns like Sierra City and Clio offer skiing in the winter, four golf courses, hiking, bicycling, antique shops, old mines and more.

Quincy, a small mountain town in the heart of the Northern Sierra's Feather River Country, is an area steeped in gold mining history. The town has just been honored for the restoration of its historic buildings.

Nevada City became an affluent boom town after gold was discovered. It retains its prosperous look with a beautifully restored downtown filled with interesting shops and tempting restaurants.

Indeed, if you want to get into the sun and away from the jangled nerves of city life, the High Sierra is just what you need.

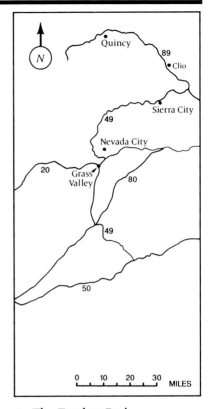

- The Feather Bed
- Grandmere's Inn
- High Country Inn
- Murphy's Inn
- Red Castle Inn
- White Sulphur Springs Ranch

The Feather Bed

542 Jackson Street
P.O. Box 3200
Quincy, CA 95971
(916) 283-0102
Credit cards: Visa, MC, AE, Diners

BUILT in 1893 in the Queen Anne style, electricity and a Greco-Roman facade were added in a turn-of-the-century renovation. The inn's seven cozy guest rooms are decorated in country Victorian wallpapers and boast special touches like a private balcony or separate sitting rooms. All rooms include private baths, most with old-fashioned clawfoot tubs and showers.

Recipe: Eggs Goldenrod, page 119

Grandmere's Inn

449 Broad Street
Nevada City, CA 95959
(916) 265-4660
Credit cards: Visa, MC

LISTED as the "Sargent House" in the National Register of Historic Places, Grandmere's Inn is a lovely three-story colonial Revival home built in 1856. The large lawns and Victorian flower garden surrounding the imposing residence make it ideal for weddings and parties. The Country French decor is elegant and fanciful. Six guest rooms feature private baths and queen size beds. A full country breakfast is served in the dining room.

Recipe: Annette's Cookies, page 190

High Country Inn

Highway 49 and Gold Lake Road
HCR2, Box 7
Sierra City, CA 96125
(916) 862-1530
Credit cards: Visa, MC

EVERY guest room at the High Country Inn features a view: of the Yuba River, of a private pond surrounded by pines and golden aspens, of the 8,600-foot Sierra Buttes. More than 20 trout-filled mountain lakes are within a 10-mile radius. A suite offers cathedral windows, antique tub and fireplace. Other activities: Skiing, golf, hiking, cycling, boating, swimming, antique shops and old mines.

Recipe: Banana Muffins, page 137

Murphy's Inn

318 Neal Street
Grass Valley, CA 95945
(916) 273-6873
Credit cards: Visa, MC, AE

BUILT in 1866 for gold baron Edward Coleman, Murphy's Inn is framed by a majestic sequoia tree standing amid well-kept grounds. A spacious veranda and manicured ivy baskets add a delightful touch. The inn features two sitting rooms with fireplaces. Eight guest rooms, three with fireplaces and six with private baths, are graced with antiques, lace curtains and floral wallpapers. A swimming spa is surrounded by a sundeck. Breakfast includes such delights as Belgian waffles, coddled eggs and hand-squeezed orange juice.

Recipe: Apple Pecan Muffins, page 134

Red Castle Inn

109 Prospect Street
Nevada City, CA 95959
(916) 265-5135
Credit cards: Visa, MC

HIGH on a forested hillside, where breezes linger on wide verandas, strains of Mozart echo through lofty hallways and chandeliers sparkle, stands the Red Castle Inn. Overlooking Nevada City since before the Civil War, the imposing 1857 Gothic Revival inn has welcomed travelers since 1964. Gourmet Magazine says: "The Red Castle Inn would top my list of places to stay. Nothing else compares with it."

Recipe: Cream Cheese Pound Cake, page 195

White Sulphur Springs Ranch

P.O. Box 136 (Highway 89)
Clio, CA 96106
(916) 836-2387
Credit cards: Visa, MC

ORIGINALLY a stage coach stop, White Sulphur Springs Ranch was built in the 1850's. Commanding a view of the lush Mohawk Valley, the ranch features an Olympic-size swimming pool, balconies and many of the original furnishings. The area offers four golf courses, horseback riding, trout fishing, biking and hiking. Just an hour from Reno or Lake Tahoe, the inn offers six guest rooms plus a cottage.

Recipes: Cranberry Bread, page 142
Praline Pumpkin Pie, page 200

Notes

Notes

Sacramento and the Gold Country

Sacramento is the hub, the spark that ignited California. Nearby Sutter's Mill in Coloma is where gold was discovered in 1849.

Today the state capital remains the hub of California. Visitors will want to see Oldtown, the Capitol, visit the shops and discover the wealth of fine food in the area. And the historic sites of Sacramento are a journey in themselves.

The Path of Gold follows Highway 49, to frontier towns like Sutter Creek, Jackson, Murphys, Sonora and Tuolumne. Photographers can spend days shooting the old towns, artifacts, historic cemeteries and buildings.

Columbia is a state-preserved Gold Rush town, complete with saloons, gold panning and mining equipment. Further south, Tuolumne is situated high on the slopes of the Sierra Nevada, at the doorway to Yosemite.

Auburn and Georgetown extend the Gold Rush aura that served as the birthplace of the Golden State.

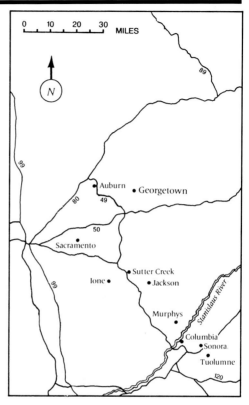

- American River Inn
- Ann Marie's Country Inn
- Aunt Abigail's
- Bear Flag Inn
- The Briggs House
- City Hotel
- Dunbar House, 1880
- The Foxes in Sutter Creek
- The Heirloom
- La Casa Inglesa
- Oak Hill Ranch
- Power's Mansion Inn
- The Ryan House
- Serenity
- The Wedgewood Inn

American River Inn

Main and Orleans Streets
P.O. Box 43
Georgetown, CA 95634
(916) 333-4499
Credit cards: Visa, MC, AE

BUILT in 1853 as a Gold Rush boarding house for miners, this restored inn features Victorian antiques, gardens, a dove aviary and a mountain stream pool complete with jacuzzi. Breakfast is served, and local wines and treats are featured in the evening. Off-street parking and handicapped facilities are offered.

Recipe: Cheese Triangles, page 160

Ann Marie's Country Inn

410 Stasal Avenue
P.O. Box DN
Jackson, CA 95642
(209) 223-1452
Credit cards: Visa, MC, Discover

THIS quaint, homey Victorian house was built in 1892 by Dr. James Wilson. The inn offers four cozy corner rooms and a tree-shaded cottage behind the main house. A Victorian-style wood stove in the parlor offers comfort in the winter; air-conditioning is offered in summer. A hearty breakfast is served either family style or in guest rooms. Special features: antique brass double bed, pot-bellied stove, clawfoot tub.

Recipe: Sour Cream Chicken Enchiladas, page 186

Aunt Abigail's

2120 G Street
Sacramento, CA 95816
(916) 441-5007
Credit cards: Visa, MC, Diners

LOCATED in downtown Sacramento, Aunt Abigail's is within walking distance of Sutter's Fort, the Almond Plaza, the Convention Center and Capitol. A fireplace and comfortable chairs highlight the large living room. A piano and games are in the sitting rooms. Guests can sit in the patio on warm summer evenings. Unique features in the five guest rooms include an iron bedstead, brass bed, Victorian armoire, and oldtime radio.

Recipes: Nutmeg Coffee Cake, page 148
Zucchini Walnut Sour Cream Waffles, page 132

Bear Flag Inn

2814 I Street
Sacramento, CA 95816
(916) 448-5417
Credit cards: Visa, MC, AE

TUCKED away in downtown Sacramento, the Bear Flag Inn was built in 1910 in California "arts and crafts" style, a rebellion against Victorian over-embellishment.   The inn showcases natural woods and features nine-foot ceilings and an arc-shaped fireplace built of rose quartz. Each of the four guest retreats offers a private bath and queen-sized bed. A large veranda, complete with porch swing, graces the front.

Recipe: Berries and Cream Belgian Waffles, page 114

The Briggs House

2209 Capitol Avenue
Sacramento, CA 95816
(916) 441-3214
Credit cards: Visa, MC, AE

THIS elegant yet homey 1901 Colonial Revival is situated a few blocks from the State Capitol. The main house offers 7 guest rooms, some featuring Tiffany lamps, four poster bed, and a private sun porch. The ivy-covered carriage house features two guest rooms. The innkeepers will share a gourmet breakfast, fireplace, sauna, spa, bicycles and lush garden.

Recipe: Cheddar Cheese Pie, page 173

City Hotel

Main Street
P.O. Box 1870
Columbia, CA 95310
(209) 532-1479
Credit cards: Visa, MC, AE

LOCATED in a state-preserved Gold Rush town, the City Hotel was established in 1856. The historic inn offers an intimate French restaurant of high repute, an award-winning wine list and the original What Cheer saloon. The unique Gold Rush hotel offers gold panning, theater productions and special events.

Recipe: Orange Chiffon Cake, page 198

Dunbar House, 1880

271 Jones Street
P.O. Box 1375
Murphys, CA 95247
(209) 728-2897
Credit cards: Visa, MC

WILLIS Dunbar, a civic leader and businessman, built this beautiful Italianate style home for his bride in 1880. The gracious home offers five rooms decorated in antiques, wood stoves, clawfoot tubs, lovely gardens and wide porches. Guests may have a full breakfast delivered to their room in a picnic basket, or join the other guests in the dining room by the fire, or in the gardens.

Recipe: Oatmeal Muffins, page 150

The Foxes in Sutter Creek

77 Main Street
P.O. Box 159
Sutter Creek, CA 95685
(209) 267-5882
Credit cards: Visa, MC, Discover

THE Foxes in Sutter Creek, originally built in 1857, offers six elegant suites, private baths, queen beds, air conditioning, wood-burning fireplaces, covered parking and morning newspaper. Gourmet breakfast cooked to order and served to your room, or garden gazebo, on silver service. Mobil rated 3 star. Named "The very best" by Don and Betty Martin in "The Best of the Gold Country". Also featured in the New York Times, Sacramento Bee, Los Angeles Times, Contra Costa Times, Stockton Record and Gourmet Magazine.

Recipe: Oatmeal Pancakes, page 128

The Heirloom

214 Shakeley Lane
P.O. Box 322
Ione, CA 95640
(209) 274-4468

A petite colonial mansion, circa 1863, The Heirloom is surrounded by an English romantic garden that includes century-old trees, magnolias, gardenias and wisteria. Guest rooms feature antiques, cozy fireplaces and balconies. Also offered are rooms in a handcrafted adobe cottage with hand-hewn woods in their natural finish. Skylights add a special touch. A French country breakfast is served.

Recipe: Apricot Almond Streusel, page 135

La Casa Inglesa

18047 Lime Kiln Road
Sonora, CA 95370
(209) 532-5822

THE shaft of the old Kincaid Gold mine lies near the center of a deep two-acre pond that accents this elegant Country English home. Located a few miles from the historic Gold Rush town of Sonora, La Casa Inglesa offers five tastefully decorated rooms, each with queen size bed and private bath. One suite boasts a whirlpool tub. All guests may enjoy a hot tub on the upper patio.

Recipe: Apple Dumplings, page 192

Oak Hill Ranch

18550 Connally Lane
P.O. Box 307
Tuolumne, CA 95379
(209) 928-4717

TWO years of restoration transformed this 1850's homestead into a Ranch Victorian inn situated on 56 acres in the old lumber town of Tuolumne. Antique guest rooms are available in the main house and in a Victorian cottage that boasts a rock fireplace. An old pump organ and player piano highlight a sitting room. A gazebo in the garden is ideal for weddings and parties.

Recipe: Crepes Normandie, page 174

Power's Mansion Inn

164 Cleveland Avenue
Auburn, CA 95603
(916) 885-1166

THIS stately mansion was originally built with the gold-mining fortune of the Power family, who spared no expense. The structure has a classic Victorian floorplan with twelve-foot ceilings, grand entrance hall with handcrafted staircase, ladies' and gentlemen's parlors and formal beamed dining room. The 15 guest rooms offer clawfoot tubs, terry robes, and brass or four-poster queen beds.

Recipe: Figs with Fruit Fondue, page 123

The Ryan House

153 South Shepherd Street
Sonora, CA 95370
(209) 533-3445
Credit cards: Visa, MC

BUILT in 1855 as a two-room house, The Ryan House was expanded several times before the turn of the century. At one time, the city planned to demolish the house, but residents objected and the historic house was saved. Each of the four rooms is decorated around the color of the antique lavatories. Handmade quilts and accessories complement the solid brass queen size beds and antique furnishings.

Recipe: Date and Nut Bread, page 143

Serenity

15305 Bear Cub Drive
P.O. Box 3484
Sonora, CA 95370
(209) 533-1441
Credit cards: Visa, MC, AE

THIS elegant 19th-century-styled house drew its name from the serenity of its six wooded acres studded with ponderosa pines, oaks and wildflowers. Four guest rooms, each with private bath, are named Rose, Daffodil, Lilac and Violet. Guests are invited to relax in the parlor, library or veranda. The inn is close to Gold Rush towns, Big Trees and Yosemite.

Recipe: Date Cake, page 196

The Wedgewood Inn

11941 Narcissus Road
Jackson, CA 95642
(209) 296-4300
1-(800) WEDGEWD
Credit cards: Visa, MC, Discover

NESTLED on five acres of pines and oak, The Wedgewood Inn is an elegant 1987 replica Victorian with wraparound porch and swing. The six guest rooms, each with private bath, are furnished with antiques and family heirlooms. Some rooms feature carved beds, bay windows, balconies and wood-burning stoves. A full gourmet breakfast is served on bone china in the formal dining room.

Recipe: Eggs a la Wedgewood, page 116

Notes

Notes

Humboldt County

The world's tallest trees, California's "Lost Coast", salmon fishing and elaborate Victorian architecture are all synonymous with Humboldt County.

Eureka, the area's largest city, boasts an Old Town full of renovated Victorian buildings, a harbor and the famous Carson Mansion.

The Victorian Village of Ferndale is a state historical landmark because of its well-preserved Main Street and homes from the late 1800's.

Visitors from all over the world arrive in Humboldt to walk among the giant redwoods in both state and national forests, to stroll along the miles and miles of beaches, to fish the mighty rivers and to visit the numerous art galleries, museums and shops.

Special events, such as the mid-summer Scandinavian Festival, the Great Arcata to Ferndale Kinetic Sculpture Race and the Rhododendron Festival, take place throughout the year.

Located just north of Mendocino County, Humboldt is linked by Highway 101 to San Francisco and Oregon, and by Highway 299 to Redding and Interstate 5.

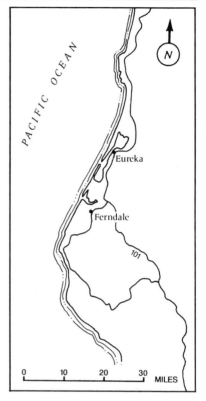

- Carter House
- The Gingerbread Mansion

Carter House

1033 Third Street
Eureka, CA 95501
(707) 445-1390

THE Carter House is a Victorian mansion modelled after a 19th century banker's home originally constructed in San Francisco and destroyed in the 1906 earthquake and fire. Innkeepers Mark and Christi Carter have given the magnificent structure a new life in Old Town Eureka. The inn, which offers views of the bay, was featured in such magazines as Bon Appetit, Travel & Leisure and Gourmet.

Recipe: Grilled Rabbit with Honey/Mustard Sauce, page 177

The Gingerbread Mansion

400 Berding Street
Ferndale, CA 95536
(707) 786-4000
Credit cards: Visa, MC

VICTORIAN elegance abounds in one of Northern California's most-photographed inns, which offers nine large, romantic guestrooms, all with private bath with shower. Each room is beautifully appointed with antiques, several featuring old-fashioned clawfoot tubs. The Fountain and Gingerbread suites each have two such tubs for his-and-her bubble baths. The inn offers four parlors, afternoon tea, bicycles, bedside chocolates, lovely English gardens.

Recipes: Bran Muffins, page 138
Lemon Bread, page 146

F ood maintains life and growth. But cooking is what determines the difference between mere nourishment and good taste. Following are recipes that will help you cook INN style.

FOOD INDEX

DESSERTS

ENTREES / SIDE DISHES

SOUPS / SALADS

Breakfast / Brunch

Baked Apples with Rice Pudding

Yield: 10 servings
Preparation time: 1 hour
Cooking time: 20-30 minutes

10 apples, any variety

For pudding:

$^2/_3$ **cup sugar**	$^1/_4$ **tsp. nutmeg**
2 **Tbsp. flour**	$^1/_1$ **to** $^3/_4$ **cup of apple meat**
1 **Tbsp. corn starch**	$2^1/_2$ **cups milk**
$^1/_4$ **tsp. salt**	3 **egg yolks**
$1^1/_2$ **cups currants or raisins**	$^1/_2$ **tsp. vanilla**
$^1/_2$ **tsp. cinnamon**	2 **cups cooked rice**

For sauce:

$^1/_4$ **lb. butter**	$1^1/_2$ **cups granola**
$1^1/_2$ **cups brown sugar**	$^1/_4$ **to** $^1/_2$ **cup honey**

Cut tops of apples approximately $^1/_2$-inch down, core and remove part of meat, leaving $^1/_4$-$^1/_2$-inch around the edge. Reserve meat.

In a heavy saucepan, combine dry ingredients.

In a bowl, mix yolks and milk. Whisk liquid ingredients into pan with dry ingredients.

Cook over medium heat, stirring constantly until mixture begins to thicken. Then let boil for approximately one minute. Remove from heat and add vanilla.

Mix rice, currants or raisins, cinnamon, nutmeg and apple meat into pudding.

Stuff apples liberally, replace tops. Bake in a sided cookie sheet or baking pan at 350° for 20-30 minutes.

Let cool slightly.

Sauce

In a saucepan, combine butter, brown sugar, granola and honey. Place on low to medium heat and cook, until ingredients are melted together. More butter may be added.

Place baked apples in a serving dish and ladle sauce over the top. Serve warm.

The Martine Inn, page 6

Baked Pears with Yogurt

Yield: 10 servings
Preparation time: 20 minutes
Cooking time: 30 minutes

       5 **large ripe pears**
       1 **cup dark brown sugar**
     ³/₄ **cup butter**
          Cinnamon
          Nutmeg
          Plain Yogurt
          Honey

   Slice pears in half, remove core and stem. Line bottom of glass baking dish with the brown sugar. Lay pears, cut side down, on brown sugar. Pour orange juice over pears and dot with butter. Sprinkle generously with cinnamon and nutmeg and a pinch of cloves. Bake at 350° for 20-30 minutes or until pears are tender.

   To serve, place pear, cut side down, in a serving dish, pour some of the brown sugar/orange juice mixture over the pear and top with a dollop of yogurt sweetened with honey.

Joshua Grindle Inn, page 73

Berries and Cream Belgian Waffles

Yield: 12 medium waffles
Preparation time: 15 minutes, plus 45 minutes for rising
Cooking time: 4 minutes per waffle

    1 pkg. dry yeast (rapid rising)
    2 cups warm milk
    4 eggs, separated
    1 tsp. vanilla
 2¹/₂ cups sifted flour
  ¹/₂ tsp. salt
    1 Tbsp. sugar
  ¹/₂ cup melted butter
      Fresh raspberries and blackberries
      Whipped cream
      Powdered sugar

Sprinkle yeast over warm milk; stir to dissolve. Beat egg yolks and add to yeast mixture with vanilla. Sift together flour, salt and sugar; add to liquid ingredients. Stir in melted butter and combine thoroughly.

Beat the egg whites until stiff, carefully fold into batter. Let mixture stand in a warm place about 45 minutes or until it doubles in bulk.

Top waffles with whipped cream. Spread berries over the whipped cream. Sprinkle with powdered sugar.

Cooking tip: Batter may be prepared the evening before serving. Just keep it refrigerated.

Bear Flag Inn, page 90

Bear Flag Inn
A Bed & Breakfast Inn

Cottage Cheese Delight

Preparation time: 5 minutes
Cooking time: 45 minutes

    1 cup milk
    1 cup flour
    1 pint lowfat cottage cheese
    6 eggs
 $^1/_2$ cup melted margarine or butter

Blend ingredients. Grease an 8" or 9" square pan. Sprinkle with 1 pound Monterey Jack cheese. Pour egg mixture over cheese and dust with crumbs. (I use my leftover blended croissant crumbs, which add a nice, buttery crunch topping).

Bake 45 minutes at 350°. Cut into squares and top with sour cream and fruit conserve or fresh berries.

I double the recipe for the inn and bake in a 9x13-inch pan for 1 hour, 15 minutes. It may be baked a day ahead and reheated in the microwave about one minute per square as needed. Leftovers make great blintzes as filling in crepes. Top with the sour cream and fruit.

The Babbling Brook Inn, page 11

115

Eggs a la Wedgewood

Yield: 6 servings
Preparation time: 15 minutes
Cooking time: 20 minutes

¹/₂ to 1 lb. bacon
12 eggs, beaten
 1 tsp. nutmeg
    Chopped parsley
¹/₂ cup sour cream
    Green onions, chopped fine
12 button mushrooms
    Cheddar cheese, grated

Chop bacon and cook until crisp; drain on paper towels.

Mix beaten eggs with nutmeg and parsley; scramble, then set aside.

In greased quiche dish, layer in the following order: egg mixture, sour cream, green onions, bacon pieces, mushrooms and cheddar cheese.

Heat oven to 300°. Bake 20 minutes or until cheese is melted. Do not overbake.

Cooking tip: This dish can be prepared the night before. Follow all directions through the layering sequence, then refrigerate. Bake in the morning.

May be served with Basil Buttered Tomatoes. Slice tomatoes and drizzle with melted butter and basil. Heat in a microwave for one minute. Do not cook. Serve on a lettuce leaf.

The Wedgewood Inn, page 101

Eggs Florentine

Yield: *12 servings*
Preparation time: *30 minutes*
Cooking time: *30 minutes*

12 eggs
12 oz. creamed cottage cheese
8 oz. feta cheese
1¹/₂ cups Swiss cheese, grated
4 Tbsp. butter, melted
2 10-oz. boxes of chopped spinach
1 tsp. nutmeg

Beat eggs, cheese, butter and nutmeg in a large bowl. Mix in the drained spinach. Place in two quiche dishes or a 9x13 baking dish.
Bake 30 minutes at 350°.

Ye Olde Shelford House, page 53

Eggs for a Gang

Yield: 12 servings
Preparation time: 15 minutes
Cooking time: 1 hour, 15 minutes

- **12 eggs, beaten**
- **2 17-oz. cans of cream style corn**
- **4 cups (1 lb.) sharp cheddar cheese, grated**
- **2 4-oz. cans of whole green chiles, drained and chopped**
- **1 Tbsp. Worcestershire sauce**
- **1 tsp. salt**
- **1/2 tsp. pepper**

Preheat oven to 325°. In a large bowl, combine all ingredients. Beat until well mixed.

Pour mixture into 9x13-inch baking dish. Place in oven and bake 1 hour, 15 minutes, or until firm to the touch.

Cooking tip: You may prepare mixture in advance. Cover and refrigerate up to 24 hours before baking.

Fairview Manor, page 14

Eggs Goldenrod

Yield: 12-14 servings
Preparation time: 30 minutes
Cooking time: 15 minutes

10-12 hardboiled eggs
   3 Tbsp. flour
   2 Tbsp. butter
   2 cups milk
   Pinch of salt and pepper
  $^1\!/_2$ pint sour cream
   2 Tbsp. Dijon mustard
   2 cups sliced mushrooms
   2 cups shredded cheese (choose two: Cheddar, Jack or Swiss)
12-14 slices of tomato
12-14 slices Canadian bacon
  6-7 English muffins, split

Dice the whites of the hardboiled eggs and set aside. Mash the yolks until crumbly, and also set aside.

In a large saucepan, melt the butter, gradually stirring in the flour, milk, and seasonings to make a white sauce. When sauce has thickened, add sour cream and mustard, stirring until blended.

Saute mushrooms in butter, pour off excess liquid, and add mushrooms to sauce. Add cheese to sauce and stir until blended. Add diced egg whites to sauce, then remove from flame, cover, and set aside.

To assemble, place tomato slice, followed by Canadian bacon slice on toasted, buttered English muffin. Spoon sauce over top, then sprinkle with crumbled egg yolk.

Garnish with paprika and a sprig of parsley.

The Feather Bed, page 77

The feather Bed

Eggs Gruyere with Savory Garnish

Yield: 6 generous servings
Preparation time: 30 minutes
Cooking time: 35 minutes, plus

        12 large eggs, slightly beaten
         2 cups grated Gruyere cheese
         4 Tbsp. butter
         1 cup heavy cream
       ¹/₂ tsp. salt
            Generous dash of white pepper
      1¹/₂ tsp. dry mustard
         2 small tomatoes
       ³/₄ cup seasoned bread crumbs
       ¹/₂ cup unsalted sunflower nuts
       ¹/₃ cup butter

Spray a 9x13-inch glass baking dish with non-stick cooking spray. Spread cheese evenly over bottom of dish and dot with butter. Mix seasonings with cream and drizzle half of mixture over cheese. Slowly pour eggs over the cheese, and drizzle with remaining cream mixture. Bake at 325° for approximately 35 minutes, or until eggs are just set.

While eggs bake, slice six ¹/₂-inch rounds of tomatoes and place on foil-lined baking sheet. Melt butter in saucepan, add crumbs and sunflower nuts, remove from heat and mix well. During last 20 minutes of baking, place tomatoes in oven on bottom shelf. After 10 minutes, remove and top with crumb mixture and return to oven. When eggs are set, remove from oven, divide into 6 portions, serve in au gratin dishes, and top with a tomato slice garnished with a sprig of parsley or an edible flower.

The Headlands Inn, page 72

Eggs Madison

Yield: 8 servings
Preparation time: 30 minutes
Cooking time: 5 minutes

- 16 eggs
- 8 avocados
- 1 head red leaf lettuce
- 1 jar salsa (use your favorite brand)
- 2 oz. parmesan cheese, grated
- 2 oz. cheddar cheese, grated
- 4 oz. sour cream
- 1 can black olives
- 1 bunch cilantro or basil
- 1 melon

Place a leaf or two of red lettuce on each plate. Place two peeled avocado halves on each plate. Poach eggs (this can be done ahead and the eggs kept warm). Place one egg in each avocado half.

Cover eggs with warm salsa. Sprinkle with parmesan cheese, then cheddar cheese. Top each with a dollop of sour cream and a black olive.

Garnish the plate with sprig of cilantro and a slice of melon. Serve with warmed tortillas.

Madison Street Inn, page 25

Madison Street Inn

Fancy Egg Scramble

Yield: 8-10 servings
Preparation time: 20 minutes
Cooking time: 30 minutes

  6 oz. Canadian bacon, diced
  ¼ cup green onions, chopped
  6 Tbsp. butter
  4 tsp. butter, melted
12 eggs, beaten
  1 cup mushrooms, sliced thin
2½ cups bread crumbs
  ⅛ tsp. paprika
  2 Tbsp. flour
  ½ tsp. salt
  ⅛ tsp. pepper
  2 cups milk
  4 oz. American cheese, shredded (no sharp cheese)

Cook bacon in 4 tsp. butter, until tender. Add beaten eggs and scramble until set, but not dry.

Prepare a cheese sauce by melting 2 Tbsp. butter. Then blend in 2 Tbsp. flour, salt and pepper. Add the milk, stir and cook until bubbly. Then stir in the cheese.

Add egg mixture to the cheese sauce. Put in a 9x13-inch baking dish. Combine 4 Tbsp. butter, bread crumbs and paprika. Sprinkle on top of mixture. Cover and chill.

Bake uncovered at 350° for 30 minutes.

The Grey Whale Inn, page 70

THE GREY WHALE INN · FORT BRAGG, CALIFORNIA

Figs with Fruit Fondue

Yield: 2 servings
Preparation time: 20 minutes

       6 fresh figs
          Fresh blueberries, blackberries or raspberries, combined to
          make 4 oz.
       6 **Tbsp. raspberry jelly**
       4 **Tbsp. heavy whipping cream**
       2 **Tbsp. raspberry liqueur**
       1 **Tbsp. powdered sugar**

Gently peel the figs with a very sharp knife. Cut each in half lengthwise. Set aside in a bowl in the refrigerator.

Carefully clean other fruit and drain. Heat the raspberry jelly until warm, then add to berries. Fold together gently and let cool to make fondue.

With a whisk, beat the cream, liqueur and sugar in a chilled bowl until thickened, but not stiff.

To serve, spread the cream evenly on two plates. Arrange the fig halves like flower petals. Spoon the fruit fondue over the figs. Garnish with candied violets or a fresh flower centerpiece with a sprig of mint.

Power's Mansion Inn, page 98

123

French Toast with Orange Butter

Yield: 8 servings
Preparation time: 15 minutes
Cooking time: 10 minutes

4 eggs
1 cup milk
$^1/_2$ tsp. cinnamon
1 tsp. vanilla
8 oz. cream cheese
1 loaf sliced, sour French bread
1 cup marmalade
    Powdered sugar

Beat eggs until frothy, add milk, cinnamon and vanilla. Set aside.

Spread soft creamed cheese on one side of French bread. Spread marmalade on one side of cheese-covered bread. Put two slices together, cheese inside. Dip in egg mixture. Cook on griddle until brown on both sides. Sprinkle with powdered sugar. Serve with Orange Butter.

Cooking tip: Cheese should be spread completely over bread to edge of crust so that a good seal can be made, and no egg batter is inside.

<u>Orange Butter</u>
8 oz. cream cheese
$^1/_2$ lb. margarine
1 lb. powdered sugar
1 small can frozen orange juice, thawed

Beat well. Can be frozen until ready to use.

Lord Bradley's Inn, page 24

German Eggs Cakes (Eierkuchen)

Preparation time: 10 minutes
Cooking time: 7-8 minutes

- ²/₃ cup flour
- ³/₄ tsp. baking powder
- ¹/₈ tsp. baking soda
- ¹/₂ cup buttermilk
- 10 large eggs, separated
- 1 tsp. vanilla flavoring
- ¹/₄ tsp. cream of tartar
- 1 Tbsp. sugar
  Unsalted butter
- 1 cup whipped cream, sweetened
- 1 Tbsp. sour cream
  Blackberries, strawberries or any hot, thickened berry sauce

In a bowl, sift together the flour, baking powder and baking soda. Add buttermilk, egg yolks and vanilla flavoring. Beat.

In a large bowl, beat egg whites, cream of tartar and sugar, until stiff. Gently fold the flour-egg mixture into the beaten egg whites.

Preheat griddle or frying pan to 300°. Brush with butter.

For each egg cake, spoon about ¹/₂ cup of batter onto griddle. Turn egg cakes over with a spatula when bottom becomes golden brown; continue cooking on second side until golden and the edges feel dry, about 7-8 minutes total.

Serve at once. Top with whipped cream/sour cream mixture and berries or hot berry sauce.

Elk Cove Inn, page 69

ELK COVE INN

Granola Crunch

Preparation time: 15 minutes
Cooking time: 45 minutes

4½ cups regular oats
½ cup wheat germ
⅔ cup sunflower seeds
½ cup sesame seeds
½ cup raw cashews
½ cup sliced almonds
⅔ cup corn oil
⅓ cup honey
1 tsp. vanilla
¼ tsp. salt

In a large bowl, combine oats, wheat germ, seeds and nuts. In a saucepan, mix together oil, honey, vanilla and salt. Cook over low heat 3 minutes. Pour over dry mixture and blend thoroughly.

Spread out in a lightly greased 15x10x1-inch pan. Bake at 300° for 45 minutes, stirring every 15 minutes.

Store in an airtight container.

Serving tip: Serve with fresh fruit and milk or over applesauce.

Agate Cove Inn, page 68

Monterey Eggs and Salsa

Yield: 10 servings
Preparation time: 10 minutes
Cooking time: 30 minutes

- 2 cups Monterey jack cheese, shredded
- 2 cups Cheddar cheese, shredded
- 4 oz. green chiles, diced and drained
- 8 oz. cottage cheese
- $^{1}/_{2}$ cup all-purpose flour
- 1 tsp. baking powder
- 10 eggs, beaten
- 4 oz. pimentos, drained and chopped

Mix cheese, cottage cheese, pimentos and chiles. Add eggs and mix well. Mix flour and baking powder, add to cheese mixture and blend completely.

Pour into well-greased muffin cups, filling them two-thirds full. bake at 350° for 30 minutes.

<u>Salsa</u>
- $^{1}/_{2}$ cup green chiles, diced
- 8 tomatoes, peeled and chopped
- 1 medium red onion, minced
- 2 bunches cilantro, chopped
- 1 tsp. oregano
  Salt and pepper to taste.

Mix all ingredients and it's ready to go.

The Martine Inn, page 6

Oatmeal Pancakes

Yield: *4 servings*
Preparation time: 15 minutes
Cooking time: 8-10 minutes

- 1 **cup old-fashioned oatmeal**
- 1 **cup buttermilk**
- 1 **jumbo egg**
- 2 **Tbsp. salad oil**
- 1/4 **cup golden raisins**
- 1/4 **cup whole wheat flour**
- 1 **Tbsp. sugar**
- 1/2 **tsp. baking powder**
- 1/2 **tsp. baking soda**
- 1/4 **tsp. cinnamon**
- 1/8 **tsp. salt**

Combine the oatmeal and the buttermilk; chill overnight. Mix together the egg, oil and raisins; add to the oatmeal mixture. Combine the whole wheat flour, sugar, baking powder, baking soda, cinnamon and salt; add to the mixture. Cook pancakes as usual.

Cooking tip: Batter will keep four days, refrigerated.

The Foxes in Sutter Creek, page 94

Parmesan Eggs

Yield: Individual serving
Preparation time: 5 minutes
Cooking time: 10-15 minutes

Butter
2 Tbsp. parmesan cheese, grated fresh
1 egg
1 Tbsp. heavy cream

Preheat oven to 350°. Butter individual ramekin, then dust with 1 Tbsp. parmesan cheese. Break one egg into ramekin. Cover with cream, then sprinkle with another tablespoon of parmesan cheese.

Bake 10-15 minutes, or until egg is bubbly and beginning to turn golden.

Belle de Jour Inn, page 39

Belle de Jour Inn

Sausage Vegetable Roll with Mustard Sauce

Yield: 3 rolls
Preparation time: 30 minutes
Cooking time: 45 minutes

- $^3/_4$ **lb. sausage**
- 1 **cup carrots, diced**
- 1 **cup asparagus, sliced**
- $^1/_4$ **cup scallions, diced**
- $^1/_2$ **cup red pepper, diced**
- $^1/_2$ **cup green pepper, diced**
- 6 **sheets phyllo dough**

Roll jelly-roll style in 6 sheets of buttered phyllo. Bake at 350° for 45 minutes.

MUSTARD SAUCE

- $^1/_2$ **cup chicken stock**
- $1^1/_2$ **cups half and half**
- $^1/_2$ **tsp. salt, or to taste**
- 3 **Tbsp. flour**
- 2 **Tbsp. butter**
- 1 **tsp. mustard**

Mix the half and half with the chicken stock and bring to a boil. Add salt. Make a paste of flour by adding hot liquid to flour. Add paste to sauce and stir thoroughly with wire whisk. Boil for two minutes, stirring constantly. Add butter and stir until it dissolves. Add mustard and stir.

The Martine Inn, page 6

Swiss Baked Eggs

Yield: 6 servings
Preparation time: 10 minutes
Cooking time: 12 minutes

6 eggs
1 cup Swiss cheese, shredded
2 Tbsp. white wine
¹/₂ cup heavy whipping cream
Dash of nutmeg

With a wire whisk, beat whipping cream for about one minute, until thickened. Add wine and nutmeg and stir in thoroughly.

Spray six ramekins with non-stick coating. Place 1 Tbsp. whipped cream on the bottom of each ramekin. Sprinkle a thin layer of cheese over cream. Break egg into ramekin over the cheese. Add another layer of whipped cream, then another layer of cheese.

Bake at 325° about 12-18 minutes, until yolks are set to taste.

Cooking tip: Any of the following items may be placed in the bottom of the ramekin for a delicious combination: Canadian bacon, tomato, green onions, or diced boiled potatoes.

Oliver House, page 63

Zucchini Walnut Sour Cream Waffles

Yield: 5-6 four-inch waffles
Preparation time: 10 minutes
Cooking time: Depends on waffle iron

1½ cups all-purpose flour
 1 tsp. baking powder
¾ tsp. baking soda
¾ tsp. salt
¼ cup chopped nuts
 2 eggs, lightly beaten
 1 cup sour cream
½ cup milk
¼ cup salad oil
½ cup zucchini, shredded

In large bowl, mix flour with baking powder, soda and salt. Add chopped nuts. In a medium-size bowl, mix eggs, sour cream, milk, oil and zucchini; blend well and pour all at once into flour mixture. Stir batter until smooth.

Bake in a preheated waffle iron according to manufacturer's directions. Top with butter and maple syrup.

Aunt Abigail's, page 89

Aunt Abigail's

Breads / Muffins

Apple Pecan Muffins

Preparation time: 15 minutes
Cooking time: 35 minutes

1¼ cups oil
2 cups sugar
3 eggs
2 tsp. vanilla
3 cups all-purpose flour
1 tsp. baking soda
1½ tsp. cinnamon
3 cups Granny Smith apples, chopped
2 cups pecans, chopped

Combine oil, sugar and eggs and cream together. Stir in vanilla. Add all dry ingredients and mix very well. Then add chopped apples and pecans. Grease and flour or spray muffin pans. Cook at 350° for 35 minutes.

Murphy's Inn, page 80

Apricot Almond Streusel

Yield: 16-18 servings
Preparation time: 20-25 minutes
Cooking time: 40 minutes

4-5 cups fresh apricots, diced	$^1/_4$ tsp. cinnamon
$^1/_4$ cup water	$1^1/_4$ cups butter or margarine
$2^3/_4$ cups sugar	2 eggs
$^1/_3$ cup cornstarch	1 cup buttermilk
$3^1/_2$ cups flour	1 tsp. almond extract
1 tsp. baking powder	$^1/_4$ cup coconut
1 tsp. baking soda	$^3/_4$ cup almonds, shaved or
1 tsp. salt	slivered

Cook apricots and water over low to medium heat for 5 minutes. Mix 1 cup sugar and cornstarch and add to apricots. Cook until thickened, then cool and set aside.

Mix together 1 cup sugar, 3 cups flour, baking powder, baking soda, salt and cinnamon. Cut in the butter to make a fine crumb mixture.

In a separate bowl, beat eggs, buttermilk and almond extract. Add to dry ingredients and stir until moistened.

Spread half of batter in a greased 9x13x2-inch baking pan. Cover with cooled apricot filling. Layer remaining batter over filling.

Make topping by cutting $^1/_4$ cup butter into $^3/_4$ cup sugar, $^1/_2$ cup flour and coconut until mixture resembles fine crumbs. Sprinkle topping over batter. Top the streusel with almonds. Bake at 350° for 40 minutes. Cool before cutting.

The Heirloom, page 95

The Heirloom
Circa 1863

Armenian Coffee Cake

Yield: 12 large or 16 medium servings
Preparation time: 10 minutes
Cooking time: 55 minutes

- 1⁵/₆ **cups flour**
- 1¹/₃ **cups sugar**
- ³/₄ **cup butter**
- 1 **tsp. cinnamon**
  Walnuts if desired
- 2 **eggs**
- 1 **tsp. vanilla**
- 1 **tsp. baking soda**
- 1¹/₂ **tsp. baking powder**
- 1 **tsp. salt**
- 1 **cup sour cream**
  Sliced apples, peaches or nectarines

Prepare the streusel ahead by mixing ¹/₃ cup sugar, ¹/₃ cup flour, ¹/₄ cup butter, 1 tsp. cinnamon and the walnuts, if desired. Mix, as for pie crust, until crumbly. Set aside.

Cream ¹/₂ cup butter and 1 cup sugar. Add eggs and beat until light. Add remaining 1¹/₂ cups flour and sour cream alternately - starting and ending with the flour. Add baking soda, salt and baking powder with last addition of flour. Blend in vanilla. Put in greased 9x5 pan. Sprinkle half the crumbled streusel evenly over the dough. Place apple, peach or nectarine slices well into the dough, about one-inch apart with the narrow side down. Cover with remaining streusel. Bake at 350° for about 55 minutes.

Chateau Des Fleurs, page 12

Chateau
Des Fleurs

Banana Muffins

Yield: 3 to 4 dozen
Preparation time: 10 minutes
Cooking time: 20 to 25 minutes

> 1 **cup butter, softened**
> 2 **cups sugar**
> 6 **very ripe bananas, gently mashed**
> 4 **eggs, well beaten**
> 1¼ **cups unbleached flour**
> 1¼ **cups whole wheat pastry flour**
> 1 **tsp. salt**
> 2 **tsp. baking soda**
> ¼ **to ½ cup of the following, alone or in any combination:**
> **oatmeal, soy granules, wheat germ, oat bran or raisins**
> **Poppy seeds, sunflower seeds or chopped nuts for topping**

Preheat oven to 350°. Cream butter and sugar together. Stir in the bananas and eggs until well blended.

Combine the two flours, salt, and baking soda. Stir into the banana mixture just until the dry ingredients are moistened. Fold in the oatmeal and/or other ingredients.

Spoon into greased muffin tins and top with seeds or nuts.

Bake at 350° for 20 to 25 minutes, or until the muffins are lightly golden and bounce back when gently touched. Cool 2 minutes, remove from tins and continue cooling on racks.

Cooking tip: These muffins freeze well.

High Country Inn, page 79

Bran Muffins

Yield: 3 dozen
Preparation time: 1 hour
Cooking time: 20 minutes

1 cup raisins	1 cup All Bran cereal
1 Tbsp. baking soda	2 cups Raisin Bran cereal
1 cup boiling water	³/₄ cup walnuts, coarsely chopped
1 cup sugar	2 Tbsp. sugar
¹/₂ cup butter	1 tsp. cinnamon
2 eggs	2 cups buttermilk
2 cups all-purpose flour	Grape-Nuts cereal
¹/₂ tsp. salt	

In a small bowl, combine raisins with baking soda and boiling water. Let cool. Cream sugar, butter and eggs in a large mixing bowl until smooth. Add flour and salt. Stir until blended. Stir in cooled raisin mixture. Stir just until mixture is combined (too much stirring causes "toughness"). Add the two cereals, walnuts, 2 tbsp. sugar and cinnamon on top. Do not stir. Cover and refrigerate (up to two weeks).

When ready to serve, add the buttermilk (well-shaken) and, once again, stir just until mixture is blended. Generously butter large (3-inch) muffin tins. Fill each ²/₃ full. Sprinkle with about ¹/₂ tsp. Grape-Nuts. Bake at 375° for 20 minutes or until done when tested.

Cooking tip: Leftover batter may be refrigerated for use in the next several days.

The Gingerbread Mansion, page 107

Breakfast Strawberry Shortcake

Yield: 12 servings
Preparation time: 45 minutes
Cooking time: 45-50 minutes

- 3 cups sifted flour
- 1 cup sugar
- 1 tsp. baking powder
- ¹/₂ tsp. salt
- 1 cup butter or margarine
- 2 eggs
- 1 tsp. baking soda
- 1 Tbsp. hot water
- 1 cup buttermilk
- ¹/₂ cup chopped walnuts
- 1 Tbsp. sugar
- 2 tsp. ground cinnamon

Sift flour into sugar, baking powder and salt. Cut in butter until all is crumbly. Set aside ¹/₂ cup of this mixture. To the rest, add eggs, one at a time, blend well after each. Dissolve baking soda in hot water. Add to buttermilk. Stir buttermilk into flour mixture. Blend till smooth. Pour ¹/₃ of batter into greased 9-inch tube pan, spread evenly.

Take the ¹/₂ cup of mixture that was set aside, add nuts, one tablespoon sugar and cinnamon, sprinkle ¹/₃ over batter, repeat twice with batter and filling, ending with filling.

Bake at 350°, 45-50 minutes.

While cake is baking, whip one pint whipping cream to a slight thickness, stopping before it peaks. Sugar to taste. Wash and dry thoroughly two baskets of strawberries. Slice and sugar to taste.

Slice coffee cake while still warm and serve with berries and cream.

Country Rose Inn, page 13

139

Buttermilk Almond Scones

Yield: Two dozen
Preparation time: 20 minutes
Cooking time: 12-15 minutes

      1 **egg**
  1¼ **cups buttermilk**
      2 **tsp. almond extract**
      4 **cups flour**
      4 **tsp. baking powder**
      1 **tsp. baking soda**
      1 **tsp. salt**
   ½ **cup sugar**
  1½ **sticks butter**
      2 **cups toasted sliced almonds, chopped**

Whisk together egg, buttermilk and almond extract.

Combine flour, baking powder, soda, salt and sugar. Cut in butter until mixture resembles coarse crumbs. Add almonds.

Add liquid ingredients to dry mixture. Mix lightly with fork until mixture clings together and forms a soft dough.

Turn dough out onto lightly floured surface and knead gently 5-6 times. Divide dough in quarters and roll out ½" thick. Cut into 6 wedges.

Bake on greased baking sheet. Brush scones with cream and sprinkle with sugar and a few sliced almonds before baking.

Bake at 425° for 12-15 minutes.

Gosby House Inn, page 4

The Gosby House Inn

Coffee Cake Supreme

Yield: 12 servings
Preparation time: 30 minutes
Cooking time: 45 minutes

½ cup butter	½ tsp. salt
½ cup sugar	1½ tsp. baking powder
½ tsp. vanilla	½ cup milk
1 egg	¼ cup chopped walnuts
1½ cups enriched flour	

For filling: Blend together and set aside:

¼ cup melted butter	1 Tbsp. cinnamon
½ cup brown sugar	¼ cup chopped walnuts
1 Tbsp. flour	¼ cup sugar-coated dates

Thoroughly cream shortening, sugar and vanilla. Add egg. Beat thoroughly. Add sifted dry ingredients, alternately with milk. Spread half the batter in greased 8″ square pan or 8″ tart pan. Cover with filling. Add remaining batter over filling, spreading it evenly to edge of pan. Top with walnuts.

Bake in moderate oven, 350° for approximately 45 minutes. Remove from pan and serve on stemmed plate, dust top of coffee cake with powdered sugar, and add flowers to center (pansies, etc.).

Cooking tip: Julia Child and her fellow judges awarded this the Best of the Best at the 1987 statewide Bed and Breakfast Conference Innkeepers Bakeoff at Santa Barbara.

The Hope-Merrill and Hope-Bosworth House, page 47

Cranberry Bread

Yield: one regular loaf or two mini-loaves
Preparation time: 5 minutes
Cooking time: 1 hour, 10 minutes

- 2 Tbsp. shortening
- 1 egg
- 1 cup sugar
- ³/₄ cup orange juice
- 2 cups flour
- 1 tsp. baking powder
- ¹/₂ tsp. baking soda
- 2 cups whole cranberries
- ¹/₂ cup nuts

Combine the shortening, egg and sugar. Combine juice, flour, baking powder, baking soda and salt. Add to shortening mixture. Fold in the cranberries and nuts.

Preheat oven to 350°. Bake for 1 hour and ten minutes.

White Sulphur Springs Ranch, page 82

White Sulphur Springs

Date Nut Bread

Yield: one loaf
Preparation time: 5 minutes
Cooking time: 1 hour

  1 **cup dates, chopped**
  1 **tsp. baking soda**
  1 **Tbsp. butter**
  ³/₄ **cup brown sugar**
  1 **cup boiling water**
  1 **egg**
  ¹/₂ **tsp. salt**
1¹/₂ **cups flour**
  ¹/₂ **cup chopped nuts**

Sprinkle baking soda over dates, then add butter and sugar. Pour boiling water over the mixture, then let cool.

Once mixture is cool, add unbeaten egg, salt, flour and nuts. Mix well and bake in greased loaf pan 1 hour at 350°.

The Ryan House, page 99

Fresh Fruit Coffee Cake

Yield: 10-12 servings
Preparation time: 15 minutes
Cooking time: 30 minutes

1¼   cup flour
1½   tsp. baking powder
 ½   tsp. salt
 ⅔   cup sugar
  1   egg, well beaten
 ⅓   cup vegetable oil
 ½   cup milk
  1   Tbsp. lemon juice
  1   tsp. cinnamon
  1   Tbsp. butter
  2   cups fruit (sliced fresh peaches or nectarines mixed with a
      small amount of lemon juice, plus a few sliced strawberries
      and a handful of blueberries. During the off season, you
      can use frozen blueberries, blackberries or dried soaked
      fruits, or applies and raisins, sprinkled with lemon juice.

Prepare the batter by combining 1 cup flour, the baking powder, salt and ⅓ cup sugar. Make a well. Beat together the egg, oil, milk and lemon juice and add to dry ingredients. Mix until smooth.

Pour into prepared 9-inch round pan with removable bottom. Place fruit over batter. When using sliced fruits, place them in a circle until covered and place sliced strawberries and blueberries evenly between slices.

Prepare the topping by mixing with a pastry blender ¼ cup flour, ⅓ cup sugar, cinnamon and butter. Sprinkle over fruit and bake in a preheated 375° oven for 30 minutes. Cool slightly before serving.

Country Meadow Inn, page 42

Hawaiian Bread

Yield: 2 loaves
Preparation time: 30 minutes
Cooking time: 1 hour

- 1 **cup vegetable oil**
- 2 **cups sugar**
- 3 **eggs**
- 1¹/₂ **cups flour**
- 1 **tsp. baking soda**
- 1 **tsp. cinnamon**
- 2 **tsp. vanilla**
- 2 **cups crushed canned pineapple, drained**
- 1 **cup grated coconut**
- 1 **cup raw carrots, grated**

Cream oil, sugar and eggs until light. Sift together flour, soda and cinnamon, then add to creamed mixture.

Gently fold in vanilla, pineapple, coconut and carrots. Divide batter in two well-greased 9x5x3-inch loaf pans. Let batter rest 20-30 minutes, then bake at 350° for 60 minutes.

Silver Rose Inn, page 65

Lemon Bread

Yield: 1 loaf
Preparation time: 1 hour
Cooking time: 50 minutes

- ¹/₂ **cup shortening**
- 1¹/₈ **cup sugar**
-   2 **eggs, slightly beaten**
- 1¹/₄ **cups flour, sifted before measuring**
-   1 **tsp. baking powder**
- ¹/₂ **tsp. salt**
- ¹/₂ **cup milk**
- ¹/₂ **cup nuts, finely chopped**
    Grated peel of one lemon
    Juice of one lemon

Cream shortening with 1 cup sugar. Mix eggs. Sift flour again with baking powder and salt. Alternately add flour mixture and the milk to shortening mixture, stirring constantly. Mix in the nuts and the lemon peel.

Bake in a greased 5x9 inch loaf pan for about 50 minutes at 350°.

As soon as the bread comes out of the oven, poke holes in the top with a fork and spoon over the topping of ¹/₈ cup sugar and lemon juice.

Cooking tip: Mix the topping just before use or it will not be smooth.

The Gingerbread Mansion, page 107

Lemon Yogurt Bread

Yield: two loaves
Preparation time: 10 minutes
Cooking time: 1 hour

      3 **cups flour**
      1 **tsp. salt**
      1 **tsp. baking soda**
   ¹/₂ **tsp. baking powder**
      3 **eggs**
      1 **cup oil**
   1³/₄ **cups sugar**
      2 **cups lemon yogurt**
      1 **Tbsp. lemon extract**

Preheat oven to 325°. Sift dry ingredients and set aside. Beat eggs in a large bowl, add oil, sugar and dry ingredients, then cream with a mixer. Add yogurt and lemon extract. Spoon into well-greased loaf pans and bake one hour.

The Napa Inn, page 62

Nutmeg Coffee Cake

Preparation time: 10 minutes
Cooking time: 1 hour, 15 minutes

3½   cups all-purpose flour
  2   cups sugar
1½   tsp. baking powder
  1   Tbsp. nutmeg
  1   tsp. salt
1½   cups milk
  1   cup (2 cubes) soft butter
  2   tsp. vanilla
  3   eggs
 ¼   cup poppy seeds
  1   cup raisins

Preheat oven to 350°. Grease a 10-inch tube or bundt pan. Combine all ingredients in large mixer bowl, except for raisins. Mix at least 3 minutes (if using a food processor, pulse several times, then mix for about 1 minute).

Pour batter into pan. Add raisins evenly over top and stir into batter. Bake for one hour and 15 minutes. Let stand for 15 minutes before removing from pan.

Cooking tip: This recipe was a prize winner in a statewide bed and breakfast bakeoff contest.

Aunt Abigail's, page 89

Nutty Oat Wheat Bread

Yield: 2 loaves
Preparation time: 2 hours
Cooking time: 35 minutes

2¹/₂ cups buttermilk
¹/₂ cup honey
¹/₃ cup butter
3¹/₂ cups unbleached flour
1¹/₂ cups rolled oats
2 pkg. active dry yeast
1 Tbsp. salt
2 eggs
2¹/₂ to 3 cups whole wheat flour
1 cup chopped nuts

In a small saucepan, heat the buttermilk, honey and butter until they are very warm (120° to 130°). In a large bowl, blend unbleached flour, oats, yeast, salt, eggs and warm liquid. Beat 3 minutes at medium speed. By hand, stir in the whole wheat flour and nuts. Put in greased bowl and brush the top with margarine. Cover and let rise for 45 to 60 minutes, until the dough doubles in size.

Stir down the dough, divide and shape into two loaves. Place in 2 greased 9x5-inch loaf pans. Cover and let rise in a warm place until it doubles, about 30 to 45 minutes.

Heat oven to 350°. Bake 25 to 35 minutes or until a deep golden brown. Remove from pan and let cool.

Healdsburg Inn on the Plaza, page 44

HEALDSBURG
INN
ON THE PLAZA

P.O. Box 1196   116 Matheson Street
Healdsburg, CA 95448 (707) 433-6991

Oatmeal Muffins

Yield: 12 small or 8 large
Preparation time: 10 minutes
Cooking time: 18-20 minutes

- ³/₄ **cup flour**
- ¹/₂ **cup whole wheat flour**
- 1 **cup rolled oats**
- ¹/₂ **cup brown sugar, firmly packed**
- ¹/₂ **tsp. baking powder**
- ¹/₂ **tsp. baking soda**
- ¹/₂ **tsp. cinnamon**
- ¹/₄ **tsp. salt**
- ³/₄ **cup buttermilk**
- ¹/₄ **cup applesauce**
- ¹/₄ **cup oil**
- 1 **egg**
- ¹/₄ **cup raisins**

Lightly spoon flour into measuring cup and level off. In large bowl, combine the flour, whole wheat flour, rolled oats, brown sugar, baking powder, baking soda, cinnamon and salt. Stir in buttermilk, applesauce, oil and egg; mix well. Fold in raisins, cover tightly and refrigerate overnight. Note: if desired, muffins can be baked immediately.

Heat oven to 400°. Grease muffin cups or line with paper cups. Fill greased muffin cups ³/₄ full for small or to the rim for large muffins. Bake at 400° for 18-20 minutes, or until a toothpick inserted into the center comes out clean.

Dunbar House, 1880, page 93

Dunbar House, 1880

Oatmeal Scones

Yield: One 7-inch round or 8 wedges
Preparation time: 5 minutes
Cooking time: 15 minutes

1¼ **cups flour**
½ **tsp. baking soda**
1 **tsp. baking powder**
½ **tsp. salt**
½ **cup sugar**
¼ **cup butter**
¼ **cup lard**
1 **cup oats**
⅓ **cup buttermilk**

Blend first seven ingredients in a food processor, until crumbly. Stir in oats.

Note: These ingredients may be mixed and kept indefinitely in refrigerator.

When ready to use, stir in the buttermilk. Pat dough into 7-inch diameter circle. Cut into 8 wedges and transfer to ungreased cookie sheet. Bake at 375° for 15 minutes.

Mangels House, page 15

MANGELS HOUSE

Oatmeal Shortbread

Yield: about 24
Preparation time: 15 minutes
Cooking time: 30-45 minutes

   1 **cup cold butter**
1¹/₂ **cups flour**
   ²/₃ **cup brown sugar, packed**
   ²/₃ **cup oatmeal**

In a food processor, mix butter, flour and sugar a few seconds until mixture looks like coarse meal. Remove lid and blade and stir in oatmeal with a spoon.

Place on very well-greased 10x15-inch pan and pat down firmly. Bake at 300° for 30-45 minutes, until golden.

Cut into squares or rectangles right out of the oven.

Seven Gables Inn, page 7

Sonoma Sunrise Bread

Yield: one loaf
Preparation time: 15 minutes
Cooking time: 55 minutes

- 6 **Tbsp. butter**
- 1 **cup sugar**
- 2 **eggs**
- 1 **Tbsp. orange peel, grated**
- 1 **tsp. baking powder**
- 1/4 **tsp. salt**
- 1 1/2 **cups flour**
- 1/2 **cup milk or cream**
- 1/2 **cup chopped nuts**

Preheat oven to 350°. Grease and lightly flour a 9x5-inch loaf pan. Mix butter and sugar until creamy. Beat in one egg at a time. Add orange peel.

Sift together the flour, baking powder and salt. Alternately blend the dry ingredients with milk into the creamed mixture. Fold in nuts and pour into pan. Bake for 55 minutes until lightly brown.

Cooking tip: For a sweeter taste, heat 1/4 cup orange juice with 1/4 cup sugar until dissolved. Pour over bread while warm.

The Hidden Oak, page 46

The Hidden Oak
A Bed and Breakfast Inn
BUILT IN 1913

Sour Cream Coffee Cake

Preparation time: 15 minutes
Cooking time: 45-50 minutes

  1 cup butter
  2 cups white sugar
  2 eggs
  1 cup (¹/₂ pint) sour cream
  1 tsp. vanilla
  2 cups flour
  1 tsp. baking powder
  ¹/₂ tsp. baking soda
  ¹/₂ cup chopped nuts
  ¹/₂ cup brown sugar
  1 Tbsp. cinnamon

Cream butter and 1¹/₂ cups sugar. Add eggs, sour cream and vanilla. Mix well and gradually add flour, baking powder and baking soda. Beat until well mixed.

To make the topping, mix together the nuts, brown sugar, ¹/₂ cup white sugar and cinnamon.

Sprinkle a small portion of topping in bottom of bundt pan. Cover with a layer of cake mixture; then alternate layers, ending with topping mixture.

Bake at 325° for 45-50 minutes, until cake is lightly browned and bounces back to the touch.

The Briar Rose, page 21

154

Two Fruit Muffins

Yield: 40
Preparation time: 30 minutes
Cooking time: 20 minutes

> 6 **cups flour**
> 3³/₄ **tsp. baking soda**
> 2 **tsp. baking powder**
> 3 **tsp. cinnamon**
> 2 **cups sugar**
> 2 **cups oil**
> 1 **15-oz. can crushed pineapple, drained thoroughly**
> 7 **bananas, mashed well**
> 5 **eggs**
> 3³/₄ **tsp. vanilla**

Thoroughly mix all dry ingredients. Add remainder of ingredients and mix just until blended. Fill greased muffin tins ⁷/₈ full. Bake at 350° for 20 minutes, until brown.

Seven Gables Inn, page 7

Whole Wheat Bread

Yield: 5 loaves
Preparation time: 40 minutes
Cooking time: 1 hour, 30 minutes

> **6** **cups water, at body temperature**
> **3** **Tbsp. yeast**
> **1** **cup honey**
> **5** **cups white flour**
> **3** **Tbsp. salt**
> **1** **cup oil**
> **10-13** **cups whole wheat flour**

Combine the water, yeast and honey. Let sit 5 minutes. Add the white flour. Let sit 20 minutes. Add the salt and oil, and mix. Add whole wheat flour until it forms a ball. Roll on floured surface. Add more flour, as needed, so the ball is not sticky. Knead for 10 minutes, then let rest in a covered bowl for 1 hour in a warm spot in the kitchen.

Butter bread pans. Cut dough into five equal parts. Bake at 350° for 1 to 1¹/₂ hours.

The Monte Cristo, page 27

The MONTE CRISTO
Circa 1875

Whole Wheat Carrot Bread

Yield: 2 large loaves or 3 small loaves
Preparation time: 5 minutes
Cooking time: 1 hour

    5 large carrots
    6 eggs
 1¹/₂ cups oil
 1¹/₂ cups brown sugar
    3 cups whole wheat flour
    3 tsp. cinnamon
 1¹/₂ tsp. salt
 3¹/₂ tsp. baking soda

Grate the carrots (bright idea: grate them in a blender with the liquid ingredients). Stir in together in a large bowl the sugar, flour spices and baking soda. Combine with the liquid ingredients and stir just until they are blended.

Bake in 2 large or 3 small loaf pans at 350° for about one hour.

Ten Inverness Way, page 33

TEN INVERNESS WAY
B E D   A N D   B R E A K F A S T

Appetizers

Cheshire Cheeze Roll

Preparation time: 10 minutes

1   8-oz. pkg. of Velveeta
¾   cups sour cream
4   oz. salsa, slightly drained
4   oz. sliced black olives
4   oz. diced green chiles, drained
½   cup cilantro, chopped
    Salt to taste

Start with a platter approximately 8x13. Between two pieces of wax paper, roll out cheese (you get better with practice) to approximately 10x8-inch. You may have to lift and reposition the wax paper several times to keep wrinkles out. On the final roll, put the edge of the paper at the edge of the cheese. In order, spread the lower ⅔ of cheese with the remaining ingredients.

Start to roll up the cheese (roll away from yourself and use your stomach to help hold). Finish the roll by bringing the top portion down over the bottom. Fold back the wax paper about 1 inch from the top and transfer the roll to the middle of the platter.

Pull off the paper and put pieces of paper towel on the ends to soak up excess liquid, cover with the other piece of wax paper and refrigerate.

Serve with a knife and your favorite tortilla chips.

The Jabberwock, page 5

The
Jabberwock

598 Laine St.
Monterey, Ca. 93940
(408) 372-4777

Cheese Triangles

Yield: 60 3-inch triangles
Preparation time: 20 minutes
Cooking time: 25 minutes

- $^1/_2$ **lb. Swiss cheese, finely grated**
- $^1/_2$ **lb. Monterey Jack cheese, finely grated**
- $^1/_4$ **cup minced green onion**
- $^1/_4$ **cup minced parsley**
- 1 **Tbsp. minced fresh dill**
- 3 **eggs**
- 1 **tsp. baking powder**
- $^1/_4$ **lb. phyllo dough sheets, cut into triangles**
- 1 **cup unsalted butter, melted**

Preheat oven to 350°. Butter baking sheet. Combine cheese, onion, parsley and dillweed in mixing bowl. Add eggs one at a time, beating well after each addition. Stir in baking powder and blend well. Place 1 heaping teaspoon of cheese mixture on each pastry strip as directed. Brush with butter. Bake 25 minutes.

American River Inn, page 87

Foccacia

Yield: 3 dozen bite-size squares
Preparation time: 10 minutes
Cooking time: 30 minutes

- 1 loaf of frozen whole wheat bread
  Olive oil
- 2 Tbsp. sea salt (coarse)
- 2 Tbsp. fresh rosemary
- 1 clove garlic, minced

Put frozen bread loaf in refrigerator to thaw overnight. Remove six hours before serving time and brush generously with olive oil. Place loaf in 9x13-inch jelly roll pan, put in a warm place and allow to rise until it is three times original size.

One hour before serving, brush with more olive oil and push the dough with your fingers until it covers the pan. Note: dough will not be smooth; it will have small indentations. Sprinkle generously with more olive oil, salt, rosemary and garlic. Bake at 350° for 25 minutes, or until golden brown. Cut with pizza cutter into 2-inch squares.

Cooking tip: You can use foccacia instead of crackers when serving cheese. It goes well with brie.

Foothill House, page 60

Soups / Salads

Chinese Cabbage Salad

Yield: 12-16 servings
Preparation time: 30 minutes

  1 cabbage, shredded
  6 green onions, chopped
$2^{1}/_{4}$ oz. sliced almonds
  $^{1}/_{2}$ cup sesame seeds
  1 package chicken Top Ramen
  $^{1}/_{4}$ cup margarine
  $^{1}/_{2}$ cup vegetable oil
  1 Tbsp. soy sauce
  $^{1}/_{4}$ cup vinegar
  $^{1}/_{3}$ cup sugar
    Salt and pepper to taste

In large frying pan, melt margarine. Crumble Top Ramen in the package and add to the margarine, along with sesame seeds and almonds. Brown slightly. Add the Top Ramen flavor packet and mix well. Remove from heat and cool.

Shred cabbage and mix with chopped onions. Mix well. Just before serving, add the cabbage to the Top Ramen mixture. Top with a dressing made from the oil, soy sauce, vinegar and sugar.

Campbell Ranch Inn, page 41

Salmon and Grilled Eggplant Salad

Yield: 4 *servings*
Preparation time: 45 minutes
Cooking time: 20 minutes

- 1/3 **cup fresh lime juice**
- 2 **Tbsp. tequila**
- 2 **Tbsp. olive oil**
- 2 **Tbsp. minced onion**
- 1/2 **jalapeno pepper, minced**
- 1/2 **tsp. salt**
  Freshly ground black pepper
- 1 **lb. fresh salmon filets**
- 4 **to 5 small Japanese eggplants**

Mix lime juice, tequila, onions, jalapenos and olive oil in a non-reactive container. Pour half of mixture over the salmon filets with skin side down, marinating for 15 minutes.

Slice the eggplants on the diagonal in 1/4-inch pieces. Brush with olive oil and grill until lightly marked. (This can be prepared on an outdoor grill on a fine mesh grill or indoors on a cast iron stovetop grill.)

Drain the marinade from the salmon filets and discard. Place the salmon, skin side down, on the grill and cook until bottom two-thirds of the filets are opaque, about 4-6 minutes, depending on the thickness of the filets. Turn filets over for another 2-4 minutes until fish just begins to flake. Remove from grill. Add salt and pepper to remaining marinade and pour over the warm filets.

Serve eggplant slices and sliced salmon filets on a bed of mixed summer greens such as arugula, mache, and red oakleaf.

Garnish with fresh tomatoes and cilantro or basil, using extra olive oil and lime juice if desired.

Huckleberry Springs, page 48

Shrimp and Rice Curry Salad

Yield: 6 servings
Preparation time: 30 minutes
Cooking time: 20 minutes for rice

1½ **Tbsp. white vinegar**
  2 **Tbsp. salad oil**
 ½ **tsp. curry powder**
 ¼ **cup onion, chopped fine**
  1 **cup celery, chopped fine**
 ¼ **cup green or red pepper, chopped fine**
  2 **cups cooked rice (short grain or pearl)**
 ¾ **cup Miracle Whip**

Marinate rice, onion and curry powder in vinegar and oil while chopping vegetables. Add remaining ingredients. Mix well and chill at least 2 hours before serving. Or make two days ahead, adding shrimp just before serving.

Scarlett's Country Inn, page 64

Tomato Dill Soup

Yield: 6-8 servings
Preparation time: 10 minutes
Cooking time: 25 minutes

- 2 **Tbsp. salad oil**
- 1 **large onion, thinly sliced**
- 1½ **Tbsp. dillweed**
- 3-3½ **lbs. ripe tomatoes, cored and sliced**
- 3 **Tbsp. tomato paste**
- 2 **14-oz. cans beef broth, regular strength**
  Salt and pepper to taste

Heat the salad oil in a 4-6 quart kettle. Add the onion and cook until limp. Stir in the dillweed, tomatoes and tomato paste. Bring to a boil, stirring often and breaking up the tomatoes. Reduce heat and cover, simmering for 15 minutes.

Whirl soup, a portion at a time, in a covered blender or processor until smooth.

In a pan, combine the tomatoes, beef broth and salt and pepper to taste.

Garratt Mansion, page 22

Turkey Breast and Artichoke Heart Salad

Yield: 8 servings
Preparation time: 15 minutes

       2 lbs. cooked turkey breast, coarsely chopped
    1¹/₂ cups marinated artichoke hearts, chopped
     ¹/₂ cup mayonnaise
       1 cup sour cream
       3 to 5 Tbsp. white wine vinegar
     ¹/₂ tsp. salt (to taste)
     ¹/₂ tsp. sugar (to taste)
       1 tsp. celery seed

Combine all ingredients and chill to let flavors mingle.
Serve in cooked, open artichokes, with silver dollar rolls.

The Mansion at Lakewood, page 26

Entrees / Side Dishes

Artichoke Black Olive Frittata

Yield: 12 pieces
Preparation time: 15 minutes
Cooking time: 35-45 minutes

- 10 eggs
- 1 pint cottage cheese
- $1/2$ cup melted butter
- 1 lb. jack or cheddar cheese, grated
- $1/2$ cup flour
- 1 tsp. baking powder
- $1/2$ tsp. salt
- 7-8 oz. artichoke hearts, packed in water, thinly sliced
- 4-5 Tbsp. chopped black olives
- 4 green onions, thinly sliced
- $1/2$ cup red pepper, chopped small
- $1^1/2$ tsp. pesto sauce

Whip eggs and cottage cheese together in a blender until smooth. Pour egg batter into a large mixing bowl and add all the other ingredients and mix thoroughly. Bake at 350° for 35-45 minutes or until eggs are just set. A 10-inch fluted quiche dish or oblong pan works well. Cut into wedges or squares and serve.

Cooking tips: There are many options to make the perfect frittata, depending on your preferences. You could use Swiss cheese. Or replace some of the jack cheese with up to $3/4$ cup of parmesan cheese. You could replace the cottage cheese with ricotta cheese. Or you could use sauteed globe onion and red pepper instead of the artichoke, olive and green onion.

Blackthorne Inn, page 31

Artichoke Frittata

Yield: 30 squares
Preparation time: 20 minutes
Cooking time: 75 minutes

  1 **32 oz. box frozen artichoke hearts**
  1 **package frozen chopped onions**
 12 **eggs**
  1 **Tbsp. Worcestershire sauce**
  1 **Tbsp. Coleman's mustard**
  2 **tsp. seasoning salt**
 2½ **cups half and half**
  3 **broken-up sourdough English muffins**
  1 **lb. grated Monterey Jack cheese**
  ½ **cup Italian seasoned bread crumbs**
  ½ **cup grated Parmesan cheese**

Defrost artichoke hearts. Chop in blender or Cuisinart. Coat 9x13-inch pan with spray shortening and spread with the artichoke hearts. Top with onions.

Blend half and half with the eggs and seasonings. Pour half over the artichokes in the pan. Blend the English muffins into the rest until smooth. Pour that over mixture and add Jack cheese. Stir to blend. Top with Parmesan and Italian bread crumbs. Sprinkle with paprika or chopped parsley as desired

Bake 1 hour, 15 minutes (or until the center is set) at 350° on center rack of oven. Cool slightly, cut into 30 squares.

The Babbling Brook Inn, page 11

Artichoke Mushroom Frittata

Yield: 6-8 squares per pan
Preparation time: 30 minutes
Cooking time: 40 minutes

   3 **eggs**
 3/4 **cup mayonnaise**
 3/4 **cup milk**
   3 **Tbsp. flour**
   2 **cups Swiss cheese**
   2 **cups jack cheese**
  16 **small artichokes, steamed**
 1/2 **lb. mushrooms**
 1/3 **cube butter**
 2-3 **Tbsp. green onions**

Beat the eggs, mayonnaise and milk. Add the flour and set aside. Shred the cheese and set aside.

Peel and slice the artichokes and layer in 2 shallow 1x9x6-inch pans greased with 1 Tbsp. olive oil.

Saute sliced mushrooms and onions in butter. Layer over the artichokes.

Mix cheese and milk mixture and divide, pouring half over mixture in each pan.

Bake 10 minutes at 400° and another 30 minutes at 350°. Slice and serve warm.

Rancho San Gregorio, page 28

171

Baked Beans

Preparation time: 5 minutes
Cooking time: 7 hours, 30 minutes

   1 lb. (two cups) small white navy beans
 ¹/₂ cup oil
   1 cup boiling water
 ¹/₂ cup catsup
   1 onion, diced
   2 Tbsp. molasses
   1 Tbsp. salt
   1 tsp. paprika
 ¹/₂ cup brown sugar

Soak beans overnight. Cook 30-45 minutes until tender, when they start cracking. Add other ingredients and bake 7 hours in a bean pot.

Forest Manor, page 61

Cheddar Cheese Pie

Yield: 6 servings
Preparation time: 15 minutes
Cooking time: 45 minutes

- 1 **pie crust**
  Cheddar cheese
- 6 **eggs**
- 1¹/₂ **cups cream**
  Salt and pepper to taste
  Mustard
  Fresh dill weed
  Green onions

Slightly bake the pie crust. Grate cheddar cheese and place in the crust, almost to the top. Combine the eggs, cream, salt and pepper, a squirt of mustard, and a pinch of dill. Chop the green onions and sprinkle on top of cheese. Pour liquid into crust. Bake at 350° for 45 minutes, or until set.

The Briggs House, page 91

Crepes Normandie

Yield: 4 *servings*
Preparation time: 30 minutes
Cooking time: 15 minutes

   1 **egg**
       Dash of salt
 ²/₃ **cup flour**
   1 **tsp. vegetable oil**
 ³/₄ **cup milk**
   1 **cup Motts chunky applesauce**
 ¹/₂ **cup raisins, soaked for ¹/₂ hour in 2 Tbsp. brandy**
       Dash of cinnamon
       Dash of cardamon
   1 **cup walnuts**
 ³/₄ **cup sour cream**
   1 **Tbsp. brown sugar**
   1 **cup blueberries or blackberries**

For the crepe batter, combine the egg, salt, flour, oil and milk. Beat to a thin consistency. Set aside.

For the filling, mix the applesauce, raisins, cinnamon, cardamon and ¹/₄ cup of the walnuts chopped very fine. Set aside.

For the dressing, mix the sour cream and brown sugar.

Cook the crepes in a crepe pan on medium heat until barely brown. Fill each crepe with 2 Tbsp. of filling and bake in a pan at 350° for 15 minutes.

After baking, top with dressing and sprinkle with berries and remaining chopped walnuts. Serve hot with a garnish of fresh fruit, with sausages or bacon.

Oak Hill Ranch, page 97

Oak Hill Ranch
BED & BREAKFAST

Croissants and Prawns

Yield: 4 servings
Preparation time: 10 minutes
Cooking time: 10-15 minutes

   4 **large croissants, cut lengthwise**
 20 **large prawns, cleaned and butterflied**
      Monterey Jack cheese, sliced
   1 **cube butter, melted**
   4 **cloves garlic, minced**
      Minced parsley
      Minced chives
      Capers to taste

Saute prawns in butter, garlic, chives and parsley, until just opaque. Place cooked prawns on bottom half of croissants and drizzle with butter mixture. Sprinkle with capers. Top with cheese and cover with top half of croissant. Bake at 350° until heated through, about 10-15 minutes.

Serve with fresh fruit platter and a sparkling wine.

Victorian Garden Inn, page 51

BED & BREAKFAST IN SONOMA
Victorian Garden Inn
316 EAST NAPA STREET
SONOMA, CALIFORNIA 95476
(707) 996-5339

Florentine Ham Rolls

Yield: 24 rolls (12 portions)
Preparation time: 1 hour
Cooking time: 30 minutes

24 thin slices of boiled ham, preferably rectangular
 2 10-oz. packages frozen, chopped spinach
 2 cups packaged cornbread stuffing
 2 cups sour cream
   Pepper to taste
 ½ cup butter
 ½ cup flour
 4 cups milk
 1 cup sharp cheddar cheese, grated
   Grated parmesan cheese
   Paprika

Cook spinach until just thawed, then drain well. Combine spinach, stuffing and sour cream. Spread a generous spoonful on each ham slice. Roll up and place seam-side-down in individual au gratin dishes or in a large casserole dish.

Melt butter in a saucepan; add flour and blend well. Add milk and continue stirring over medium-high heat until thick. Add cheese and remove from heat. Stir until all the cheese is melted. Pour evenly over the ham rolls. Sprinkle with parmesan cheese and paprika.

Bake at 350° for 20 minutes, covered loosely with foil and then remove foil and continue baking another 10 minutes uncovered.

Cooking tip: Cream sauce can be prepared ahead and refrigerated.

The Headlands Inn, page 72

Grilled Rabbit with Honey/Mustard Sauce

Preparation time: 24 hours to marinate
Cooking time: 40 minutes

    1 fresh rabbit, cleaned and cut
  ¼ cup honey
    4 oz. Grey Poupon mustard
    1 cube unsalted butter
       Olive oil
 3-4 cups wine
    6 cloves garlic, crushed
    1 cup tamari (soy sauce)
       Fresh rosemary, uncut

To prepare marinade, mix wine, garlic, tamari and rosemary.

Marinate rabbit 4 to 24 hours, turning occasionally. Save the marinade. In a roasting pan, pre-cook the rabbit for 30 minutes at 350°. Heat grill and cook rabbit until done - approximately four minutes per side.

To prepare Honey/Mustard Sauce, strain marinade to remove rough herbs. Reduce sauce over high heat until it is about half of its original volume; remove. Add honey and mustard. Whip sauce and slowly add butter, piece by piece (the sauce should still be warm enough to melt butter added in small portions). Drizzle sauce over rabbit and serve.

Carter House, page 106

177

Huevos Mexicanos

Yield: 12 servings
Preparation time: 15 minutes
Cooking time: 30-45 minutes

- 10 **corn tortillas, cut into eighths**
- 2 **Tbsp. butter**
- 12 **eggs**
- 1 **cup red salsa**
- ¹/₂ **cup green onions, chopped**
- 1 **cup sour cream**
- 2 **cups grated cheese, either cheddar or jack**

Preheat oven to 275°. Butter a 9x12 glass baking dish.
Saute tortilla pieces in butter until soft but not crisp.
Lightly scramble the eggs.
In the baking dish, make a layer of tortillas, then scrambled eggs, salsa, onions, sour cream and cheese. Repeat the layers.
Cover with foil and bake 30-45 minutes, until cheese is melted. Cut into squares and serve.

Serving tip: Delicious with refried beans. David Rosengarten of "Wine and Food Companion" calls this dish "THE way to start the day."

Camellia Inn, page 40

Ray & Del Lewand — Innkeepers
Since 1869 **Camellia Inn**
The Elegance of Yesteryear - Bed & Breakfast

Leg of Lamb with Pistachio Nut Stuffing

Yield: 8 servings
Preparation time: 30 minutes
Cooking time: 90 minutes

6-7 lb. leg of lamb, boned	**Pistachio Nut Stuffing**
Salt	**(recipe follows)**
Black pepper	**Sherry Glaze**
2 garlic cloves, minced	**(recipe follows)**
1½ tsp. dried rosemary	

Preheat oven to 350°. Lightly pound the leg of lamb. Spread the prepared Pistachio Nut Stuffing evenly over the leg. Roll and tie the leg. Place the lamb on a rack in a roasting pan and season with salt and pepper.

Make a paste with the garlic and rosemary and rub it into the lamb. Bake the lamb for 1½ hours, or until a meat thermometer registers 135° for medium rare. Roast longer if desired. Baste lamb frequently with the warm Sherry Glaze. Remove the meat and let it stand for 10 minutes before carving.

Pistachio Nut Stuffing

⅔ cup golden raisins	**½ cup parsley, chopped**
½ cup dry sherry	**⅔ cup fresh bread crumbs**
1 cup pistachio nuts, shelled	**1 tsp. dried rosemary**
4 cloves garlic, chopped	**1 large egg, beaten**

Soak the raisins in sherry for 30 minutes. Drain, reserving both raisins and sherry. Coarsely chop ¾ cup of the pistachios and add the raisins, garlic, parsley and bread crumbs. Add the egg to bind. Stir in the remaining nuts.

Sherry Glaze

Sherry reserved from stuffing preparation
¼ cup butter
1 tsp. dried rosemary
¼ cup apple jelly

Combine ingredients in a small saucepan.   Heat, stirring frequently, until the jelly melts.

The Estate Inn, page 43

Oriental Ginger Pork

Yield: 4-6 servings as main dish; 8-10 as appetizer
Preparation time: 20 minutes
Cooking time: 10 minutes

       2 lbs. boneless pork loin, thinly sliced
       1 Tbsp. fresh ginger, grated
    ¹/₄ cup soy sauce
    ¹/₄ cup sake
       1 Tbsp. garlic, minced
   1¹/₂ Tbsp. brown sugar
           Vegetable oil

Combine ginger, soy sauce, sake, garlic and brown sugar. Marinate pork slices at least ten minutes, then remove pork, saving the marinade.

Brush oil in large skillet, then saute pork on moderate heat until brown on both sides, adding oil as needed.   Remove meat from skillet once it is browned.

When all the meat has been browned, pour the marinade in the skillet and return the meat. Cook on medium heat until glazed. Do not overcook. To serve, sprinkle with minced green onion.

Serving tip: Serve with rice and an Oriental vegetable, such as snow peas with water chestnuts. Makes a great appetizer.

Harbor House Inn by the Sea, page 71

Marinated Pork Tenderloin, Orange Sauce

Yield: 8-10 servings
Preparation time: 45 minutes
Cooking time: 20 minutes

   3 pork tenderloins
 ¹/₂ cup lemon juice
 ¹/₂ cup soy sauce
 ¹/₂ cup Marsala (or red) wine
 ¹/₂ tsp. pressed garlic
   2 tsp. ground ginger
 ²/₃ cup sugar
   1 Tbsp. cornstarch
 ¹/₂ tsp. salt
  20 whole cloves (tied in cheesecloth)
 ¹/₂ tsp. cinnamon
   1 Tbsp. orange rind
   1 cup orange juice

Prepare marinade by combining lemon juice, soy sauce, wine, garlic and ginger. Marinate the pork overnight.

Prepare orange sauce by combining in a pot the sugar, cornstarch, salt, cloves, cinnamon, orange rind and orange juice. Cook over medium heat until thick and clear. Remove cloves and orange rind, and remove from heat. Cover pot.

Barbecue the pork tenderloins on hot fire, about 12-20 minutes, depending on thickness and desired doneness. Top with orange sauce and garnish with orange slices.

Madison Street Inn, page 25

Madison Street Inn

Potato Pie

Yield: 12-16
Preparation time: 30 minutes
Cooking time: 40 minutes

  10 eggs
1¹/₂ tsp. onion powder
 ¹/₄ tsp. garlic powder
1¹/₂ cups cottage cheese
 10 small to medium potatoes, cooked and cubed
 ²/₃ cup bacon bits
 12 oz. Jack cheese, grated
      Bunch of scallions, chopped

In a blender, mix eggs, onion powder, garlic powder and cottage cheese. In a large bowl, combine with the other ingredients. Spray two 10-inch pie plates with a non-stick spray coating and divide ingredients evenly. Bake at 350° for 40 minutes or more, until set.

Cooking tip: Can be prepared the day before and baked the next morning.

Beazley House, page 58

Poulet Saute Aux Olives de Provence

Yield: 4 servings
Preparation time: 15 minutes
Cooking time: 35 minutes

     1 **chicken, cut up**
        Flour
     6 **Tbsp. olive oil**
     1 **green pepper, seeded and chopped**
     1 **red pepper, seeded and chopped**
     2 **cloves garlic, minced**
   4-6 **anchovy filets, minced**
   ¼ **tsp. thyme**
   ¼ **tsp. basil**
   ¼ **tsp. marjoram**
        Salt and pepper to taste
   ⅔ **to 1 cup Nicoise olives**

Dredge chicken in flour and brown in olive oil. Remove to warm platter.

In the same pan, cook peppers, garlic, anchovies, thyme, basil, marjoram, salt and pepper. Return chicken to pan, cover, and cook 10 minutes.

Uncover, add olives, and turn chicken. Recover and cook another 20 minutes.

Madrona Manor, page 49

183

Sausage-Biscuit Pinwheels

Yield: 50-60
Preparation time: 20 minutes
Cooking time: 15 minutes

  1½ **to 2 lbs. bulk pork sausage**
  4 **cups flour**
  1 **tsp. baking powder**
  ½ **tsp. baking soda**
  ¼ **tsp. salt**
  1 **cup shortening**
  1½ **cups buttermilk**

Sift 3½ cups flour into a large mixing bowl. Make a well in the center and add the baking powder, soda, and salt. Mix well, then cut in the shortening. Add the buttermilk and mix well. Add last ½ cup of flour and blend completely until smooth, but not sticky.

Wrap dough in waxed paper and chill for 1 hour; that will make it easier to work with.

Divide the dough in halves. Roll out each half on a floured surface to a ¼-inch thickness and roughly an 18x8-inch rectangle. Spread each rectangle thinly with sausage. Leave ½ inch on one long edge free of sausage so it will seal when rolled. Roll each rectangle into log-shaped cylinder. Chill at least 30 minutes so that logs will cut cleanly.

Preheat oven to 450°.

Cut logs in ½-inch rounds. Place ½-inch apart on ungreased baking sheet. Bake 15 minutes, or until sausage is cooked and dough is golden.

Cooking tips: Rolled, uncut logs can be prepared a day ahead and refrigerated. Note: if sausage is fatty, bake on a broiling pan so the grease will drain.

Goose & Turrets, page 23

184

Sausage Frittata

Yield: 10 servings
Preparation time: 15 minutes
Cooking time: 20 minutes

    1 lb. Italian sausage
    1 medium red onion, chopped
    1 medium green pepper, chopped
    3 small zucchini, diced
   18 eggs
    1 tsp. dried basil
    1 tsp. dried oregano
 1½ cup jack cheese, grated
       Salt and pepper

Remove sausage from casing and saute until no longer pink. Saute onion and green pepper until soft, then add zucchini and cook slightly.   Put vegetables and sausage into two shallow 1-quart casseroles sprayed with a non-stick spray coating.

In another pan, cook scrambled eggs until they are still very runny, then add herbs and salt and pepper to taste. Pour egg mixture over vegetable mixture and sprinkle with cheese. Bake at 350° about 20 minutes or until eggs are set. Cut into wedges to serve.

Chestelson House, page 59

Chestelson House

Sour Cream Chicken Enchiladas

Yield: 1 dozen
Preparation time: 45 minutes
Cooking time: 30 minutes

       3 cans cream of chicken soup
     ³/₄ cup sour cream
       1 small can diced green chiles
     ¹/₂ tsp. salt
       1 tsp. cumin
     4-5 tsp. hot salsa, to taste
       2 cups cheddar cheese, grated
       3 cups cooked chicken
       1 cup green onions, chopped
       1 dozen large flour tortillas

In a saucepan, combine soup, sour cream, chiles, salt, cumin and salsa. Stir over medium heat until smooth. Remove from heat.

To make the filling, mix the cheese, chicken and green onions.

Spread thin layer of sauce in large Pyrex baking dish. Place one-twelfth of the filling in each tortilla, add 1 heaping Tbsp. of sauce, roll tortilla and place in dish. Cover all the rolled tortillas with the remaining sauce, add a little grated cheese over top, cover with foil and bake 30 minutes at 350°. Garnish with sour cream and chopped green onions.

Ann Marie's Country Inn, page 88

Special Morning

Yield: 12
Preparation time: 5 minutes
Cooking time: 45 minutes

- 2 lb. hash-brown potatoes
- 16 oz. cream of celery soup
- 16 oz. cream of potato soup
- 10 oz. diced ham
- 1 lb. cheddar cheese, grated

Mix all ingredients in a bowl. Put in a buttered 9x12 Pyrex dish and bake uncovered at 350° for 45 minutes.

Madison Street Inn, page 25

Madison Street Inn

Zucchini Frittata

Yield: 6-8 servings
Preparation time: 10 minutes
Cooking time: 20 minutes

- 6 eggs
- 2 Tbsp. cold water
- ¼ tsp. oregano
- 1 zucchini
- 1 shallot or green onion
- 1 tomato
- 1 stalk celery
- 2 oz. parmesan cheese
- 2 Tbsp. olive oil

Slice the zucchini lengthwise, then into thin slices crosswise. Chop the shallot, tomato and celery. Heat 1 Tbsp. of the olive oil in a 12-inch non-stick skillet and saute the vegetables about 6 to 8 minutes, but do not brown. Beat the eggs and 2 Tbsp. of water and add the sauteed vegetables, and oregano. Heat the remaining olive oil over medium high and pour in the egg mixture. Sprinkle with cheese.

Cook until the egg is just set in the center. With a spatula, lift the edges of the egg pancake to allow the egg to run to the sides. Peek at the bottom of the pancake and when brown, put a dinner plate over the skillet and flip the frittata onto the plate. Slide the frittata back into the pan to cook the unbrowned side lightly. Remove from heat.

Serving tip: Warm, pie-shaped wedges can be topped with salsa or sour cream for added zest. Or try it in smaller pieces, at room temperature, as an appetizer.

Holly Tree Inn, page 32

Desserts

Annette's Cookies

Yield: 7-8 dozen
Preparation time: 15-20 minutes
Cooking time: 15-20 minutes

    2 cubes sweet butter, softened
  ½ cup brown sugar, packed
  ½ cup white sugar
  ½ cup yogurt
  ½ tsp. cream of tartar
  2 tsp. vanilla
2½ cups whole wheat pastry flour
  1 tsp. baking soda
  ½ tsp. salt
  1 12-oz. package chocolate chips (or 1½ cups raisins)
  4 cups granola or trail mix or assorted nuts

Mix together the butter, brown sugar and white sugar. Add yogurt, cream of tartar, vanilla; and mix. Add flour, baking soda and salt; and mix. Add chocolate chips (or raisins) and either granola, trail mix or nuts. Place Tbsp. size dough on ungreased cookie sheet. Bake at 375° for 15 or 20 minutes until golden.

Cook's note: This recipe was requested by Bon Appetit Magazine.

Grandmere's Inn, page 78

Grandmère's
BED & BREAKFAST
Inn

Apple Crisp

Yield: 12 servings
Preparation time: 20 minutes
Cooking time: 1 hour

10-12 **apples**
       Handful of golden raisins
       Juice of ¹/₂ lemon
 ¹/₂ **cup sugar**
 ¹/₂ **cup brown sugar**
 ¹/₂ **tsp. nutmeg**
 ¹/₂ **tsp. cinnamon**
 ¹/₄ **tsp. salt**
 ³/₄ **cup flour**
 ¹/₂ **cup butter**
  1 **cup granola**

Sift dry ingredients and cut in butter until all is combined. Add granola last. Set aside.

Peel, core and slice 10-12 apples (enough to fill shallow glass casserole dish). Sprinkle with a handful of golden raisins. Squeeze ¹/₂ lemon and add it to ¹/₂ cup water and pour it over the apples. Sprinkle topping over the apples evenly.

Cover the casserole and bake at 350° for ¹/₂ hour then bake uncovered ¹/₂ hour. Crust will be crisp on top and will have partially seeped down through the apples, flavoring them and binding them slightly together.

Whale Watch Inn, page 74

Apple Dumplings

Yield: 6
Preparation time: 1 hour
Cooking time: 35 minutes

1½ **cups sugar**
1½ **cups water**
 ¼ **tsp. cinnamon**
 ¼ **tsp. nutmeg**
6-8 **drops red food coloring**
 3 **Tbsp. butter or margarine**
 2 **cups flour**
 2 **tsp. baking powder**
 1 **tsp. salt**
 ⅔ **cup shortening**
 ½ **cup milk**
 6 **red or golden delicious apples, pared and cored**

To make a syrup, combine sugar, water, cinnamon, nutmeg and food coloring. Bring to a boil, then remove from heat and add butter.

To make the pastry, sift dry ingredients together; cut in shortening until mixture resembles coarse crumbs. Add milk all at once and stir just until flour is moistened. Roll dough into an 18x22-inch rectangle about ¼-inch thick. Cut six 6-inch squares.

Place a whole apple in each square and sprinkle apple generously with sugar, cinnamon, and nutmeg. Dot with butter. Moisten edges of squares. Fold corners to center and pinch edges together. Place 1-inch apart in ungreased baking pan. Pour syrup over dumplings. Bake at 375° for 35 minutes or until apples are done. Serve warm.

La Casa Inglesa, page 96

Applesauce Cake

Preparation time: 15 minutes
Cooking time: 65-70 minutes

2½ cups all-purpose flour
2 cups sugar
1 tsp. baking soda
1½ tsp. baking powder
2 tsp. salt
1 tsp. ground cinnamon
¾ tsp. ground cloves
¾ tsp. allspice
2 cups applesauce
½ cup melted butter
4 eggs, separated
¼ cup cold water
1 cup raisins
1 cup walnuts, chopped fine
1½ cups sweet chocolate chips

Preheat oven to 360°. Grease and flour a 13x9x2-inch baking pan (Pyrex works best).

Put all ingredients into large mixing bowl, except for egg whites and ½ cup sugar. Beat approximately 7 minutes on medium speed, then 5 minutes on high speed.

Beat egg whites with sugar until very stiff. For best results, chill egg whites and mixing bowl in freezer for a few minutes. Fold egg mixture into batter.

Bake for 65-70 minutes, or until toothpick comes out clean.

Ridenhour Ranch House Inn, page 50

Caramelized Pears

Yield: 8
Preparation time: 10 minutes
Cooking time: 1 hour

4 Danjou pears, halved, cored and peeled
8 heaping Tbsp. brown sugar
8 pats of butter
¹/₂ cup heavy cream

Preheat oven to 350°. Place 8 pear halves face down in glass baking dish. Top each half with one heaping Tbsp. of brown sugar and one pat of butter. Bake for 45 minutes. Pour cream over top and bake an additional 15 minutes.

With spatula, remove pears and place on serving dishes. Whisk the sauce with a fork until smooth, then spoon over pears.

Serving tips: Garnish with a sprig of mint for breakfast or serve with vanilla ice cream for dessert.

The Ambrose Bierce House, page 57

Cream Cheese Pound Cake

Yield: 16-20 slices
Preparation time: 40 minutes
Cooking time: 1 hour, 30 minutes

1½ cups chopped pecans
 1 8-oz. package cream cheese, softened
 3 cups sugar
 3 cups sifted cake flour
1½ cups softened butter
 6 eggs
   Dash of salt
1½ tsp. vanilla

Sprinkle ½ cup pecans in a greased and floured 10-inch tube pan, then set aside. Cream butter and cream cheese; gradually add sugar, beating until light and fluffy. Add eggs one at a time, beating well after each. Add flour and salt, stirring until combined. Stir in vanilla and 1 cup pecans. Pour into prepared pan.

Bake at 325° for 1½ hours or until a wooden pick comes out clean. Cool in pan 10 minutes, remove and cool on a rack.

Red Castle Inn, page 81

· RED · CASTLE · INN ·

Date Cake

Yield: 16 slices
Preparation time: 15 minutes
Cooking time: 25-30 minutes

  1 **cup brown sugar**
  1 **cup white sugar**
  3 **cups flour**
  ¹/₂ **tsp. salt**
  1 **cup shortening**
  1 **cup dates, sliced**
  ³/₄ **cup chopped walnuts**
  1 **cup sour milk**
  1 **tsp. baking soda**

Mix together the brown sugar, white sugar, flour and salt. Cut in the cup of shortening. Put aside one cup of this mixture for use as a topping.

Add the rest of the ingredients and stir until moist throughout.

Spread in two 8 or 9-inch greased cake pans. Cover with reserved topping. Bake at 250° for 25 minutes.

Serving tip: This eggless cake freezes well. Topped with whipped cream, it makes a good dessert.

Serenity, page 100

Serenity
a bed & breakfast inn

Irresistible Cookies

Yield: 200
Preparation time: 15 minutes
Cooking time: 10 minutes

2 cups butter	2 tsp. baking soda
2 cups brown sugar	2 cups chocolate chips
2 cups white sugar	3 cups raisins
4 eggs	3 cups nuts
2 tsp. vanilla	2 cups old-fashioned
4 cups flour	rolled oats
2 tsp. baking powder	3 cups orange/almond
2 tsp. salt	granola mix

Blend the butter with the two sugars until creamy. Add the eggs and vanilla and beat until well mixed.

Sift the flour, baking powder, salt and baking soda. Add to egg mixture and beat well.

Stir in the remaining ingredients.

When well mixed, shape into golf ball size and bake on ungreased cookie sheet, 375° for 8-10 minutes or until barely golden. Best when slightly undercooked and warm from the oven.

Makes lots for you, but they go fast from the tea cart here. Dough keeps well when refrigerated. Bake as need·d.

The Babbling Brook Inn, page 11

The
Babbling
Brook
Inn

Orange Chiffon Cake

Yield: 12-15 servings
Preparation time: 20 minutes
Cooking time: 55 minutes

- **5** **cups sifted cake flour**
- **3** **cups sugar**
- **2** **Tbsp. baking powder**
- **2** **tsp. salt**
- **1** **cup salad oil**
- **10** **egg yolks**
- **1¹/₂** **cups orange juice**
   Zest of 6 oranges
- **2** **cups egg whites (15-16)**
- **1** **tsp. cream of tartar**

Sift together in a well the flour, baking powder, sugar and salt. Add the beaten egg yolks, oil and orange juice. Beat until smooth. Add the whites, which have been beaten to a very firm peak, with the cream of tartar. Fold together and pour into oiled pans.

Bake 55 minutes at 325°. Turn the oven up to 350° for 10 minutes before removing. Cool, turn out, dust with powdered sugar. Serve with whipped cream fraiche, candied orange section, and ice cream.

City Hotel, page 92

City Hotel
Est. 1856

Peach Cobbler, Strawberry-Rhubarb Sauce

Yield: 12 servings
Preparation time: 30 minutes
Cooking time: 30 minutes

6 cups peaches, sliced	1 to 1¼ cups milk or cream
1⅓ cups sugar	1 Tbsp. cinnamon
2 eggs, beaten	1 lb. rhubarb
3½ cups flour	1 basket strawberries
1 tsp. salt	½ cup apple juice
2 Tbsp. baking powder	¾ cup brown sugar
12 Tbsp. butter (1½ cubes)	

To prepare sauce trim and cut rhubarb into 1-inch pieces. Add apple juice and bring to boil. Simmer until tender. Add strawberries (if large, cut into halves) and simmer until berries are tender. Add brown sugar to taste and mix well over heat. Extra sauce may be prepared and frozen.

To prepare cobbler combine and heat peaches, sugar, and 2 beaten eggs. Do not boil. Set aside.

In separate container prepare dough by combining sifted flour, salt, baking powder, and an additional 2 Tbsp. of sugar. Cut in 12 Tbsp. chilled butter with pastry blender and gradually add milk or cream. The dough should be the consistency of thick biscuit batter.

Place hot fruit mixture in an ungreased 9x13-inch glass baking dish. Spoon dough over it and drizzle with 2-4 Tbsp. butter, 2 Tbsp. sugar, and 1 Tbsp. cinnamon. Bake in preheated 425° oven about 30 minutes or until cobbler turns a golden brown. Place in small bowls and spoon strawberry-rhubarb sauce over individual servings.

Serve warm. May be reheated in microwave if desired.

Heart's Desire Inn, page 45

HEART'S DESIRE INN
3657 Church Street
P.O. Box 857
Occidental, CA 95465
(707)874-1311
A Country Bed and Breakfast

Praline Pumpkin Pie

Preparation time: 20 minutes
Cooking time: 40-45 minutes

- ²/₃ cup nuts
- 1¹/₃ cups brown sugar
- ¹/₄ cup butter
- 2 eggs, well beaten
- 1 16 oz. can pumpkin
- ¹/₈ tsp. mace
- 1 Tbsp. flour
- ¹/₄ tsp. cloves
- ¹/₂ tsp. salt
- ¹/₂ tsp. ginger
- ¹/₂ tsp. cinnamon
- 1 unbaked pie shell
- 1 cup light cream or evaporated milk

Combine the nuts, ²/₃ cup brown sugar and butter. Press the mixture into the bottom of an unbaked pie shell. Bake at 450° for 10 minutes, then let the shell cool.

Combine the rest of the ingredients and slowly pour into cooled pie shell. Bake at 325° for 40-45 minutes.

White Sulphur Springs Ranch, page 82

White Sulphur Springs

———— RANCH ————
BED AND BREAKFAST

Raspberry and Blackberry Biscuit Pudding

Yield: 6 servings
Preparation time: 15 minutes
Cooking time: 1 hour, 30 minutes

- 1½ cups raspberries, sugared
- 1½ cups blackberries, sugared
- 8 biscuits
- 2 cups heavy cream
- 2 cups milk
- 4 eggs, plus 1 yolk
- 2 cups sugar
- 2 tsp. vanilla extract
- 2 Tbsp. Frangelico liqueur

Butter well two 9-inch round cake pans, 1½ inches deep. Arrange half the amount of each berry in bottom of pans. Cover with a layer of crumbled biscuits (2 biscuits per pan). Arrange second layer of berries in each pan, then cover with remaining crumbled biscuits.

To prepare a custard mixture, combine eggs, sugar, vanilla, and liqueur and mix well. Then add cream and milk, and mix well.

Pour custard mixture over biscuit pans. You should have enough to fill both pans. Pat down the biscuits a little so that all the biscuits are wet.

Put about a ½-inch of water in a large holding pan. Place cake pans in the water bath and bake at 325° for 1½ hours.

Let pudding cool, cover with plastic wrap and refrigerate before serving.

Vintage Towers, page 52

ADDITIONAL BBINC INNS

MARIN
Roundstone Farm B & B
P.O. Box 217
Olema, CA 94950
415-663-1020

MENDOCINO
Avalon House
561 Stewart Street
Fort Bragg, CA 95437
707-964-5555

Greenwood Lodge
5910 South Highway 1
Elk, CA 95432
707-877-3422

Noyo River Lodge
500 Casa Del Noyo Drive
Fort Bragg, CA 95437
707-964-8045

The Toll House Inn
P.O. Box 268
Booneville, CA 95415
707-895-3630

Trinidad B & B
P.O. Box 849
Trinidad, CA 95570
707-677-0840

MONTEREY
Old St. Angela Inn
321 Central Avenue
Pacific Grove, CA 93950
408-372-3246

The Sandpiper Inn at the Beach
2408 Bayview at Martin Way
Carmel, CA 93923
408-624-6433

NAPA
Bartels Ranch
1200 Conn Valley Road
St. Helena, CA 94574
707-936-4001

The Pink Mansion
1415 Foothill Boulevard
Calistoga, CA 94515
707-942-0558

Pygmalion House
331 Orange Street
Santa Rosa, CA 95401
707-526-3407

Villa St. Helena
2727 Sulphur Springs Avenue
St. Helena, CA 94574
707-963-2515

Zinfandel House
1253 Summit Drive
Calistoga, CA 94515
707-942-0733

SACRAMENTO
The Gate House Inn
1330 Jackson Gate Road
Jackson, CA 95642
209-223-3500

Gold Quartz Inn
15 Bryson Drive
Sutter Creek, CA 95685
209-267-9155

Harkey House B & B
212 C Street
Yuba City, CA 95991
916-674-1942

Oak Meadows Too
P.O. Box 619
Mariposa, CA 95338
209-742-6161

Windrose Inn
1407 Jackson Gate Road
Jackson, CA 95642
209-223-3650

Wine and Roses Country Inn
2505 W. Turner Road
Lodi, CA 95242
209-334-6988

Pleasure Point
2-3665 East Cliff Drive
Santa Cruz, CA 95062
408-475-4657

SAN FRANCISCO BAY AREA

Archbishops Mansion
1000 Fulton Street
San Francisco, CA 94117
415-563-7872

Best House B & B
1315 Clarke Street
San Leandro, CA 94577
415-351-0911

Mill Rose B & B Inn
615 Mill Street
Half Moon Bay, CA 94019
415-726-9794

Old Thyme Inn
779 Main Street
Half Moon Bay, CA 94019
415-726-1616

SANTA CRUZ

Apple Lane Inn
6265 Soquel Drive
Aptos, CA 95003
408-475-6868

Chateau Victorian
118 First Street
Santa Cruz, CA 95060
408-458-9458

Cliff Crest
407 Cliff Street
Santa Cruz, CA 95060
408-427-2609

New Davenport B & B
31 Davenport Avenue
Davenport, CA 95017
408-425-1818

HIGH SIERRA

Annie Horan's B & B
415 W. Main Street
Grass Valley, CA 95945
916-272-2418

The Chichester House
800 Spring Street
Placerville, CA 95667
916-626-1882

Clover Valley Mill House
P.O. Box 928
Loyalton, CA 96118
916-993-4819

SONOMA

Gaige House
13540 Arnold Drive
Glen Ellen, CA 95442
707-935-0237

Glenelly Inn
5131 Warm Springs Road
Glen Ellen, CA 95442
707-996-6720

Grape Leaf Inn
539 Johnson Street
Healdsburg, CA 95448
707-433-8140

Haydon House
321 Haydon Street
Healdsburg, CA 95448
707-433-5228

The Raford House
10630 Wohler Road
Healdsburg, CA 95448
707-887-9573

The Bed and Breakfast Innkeepers of Northern California
P.O. Box 7150
Chico, CA 95927

800-284-INNS
916-894-6701
FAX 916-894-0807

Please send ____ copies of Cooking and Traveling Inn Style at $12.95 each.

Add $2.00 postage and handling for the first book ordered and $1.50 for each additional book.

Please charge my
☐ Visa
☐ Master Card   #-_____
☐ Discover Card   Exp. Date_____

I have enclosed a check in the amount of $_____ payable to Bed and Breakfast Innkeepers of Northern California.

Name   _____

Address_____

City   _____   State _____   Zip _____

☐ This is a gift. Send directly to:

Name   _____

Address_____